IMAGES *of our Past*

HALIFAX
and
TITANIC

John Boileau

NIMBUS
PUBLISHING

Nimbus Publishing Limited
3731 Mackintosh St
Halifax, NS B3K 5A5
(902) 455-4286
nimbus.ca

Printed and bound in Canada

Author photo: Mark Doucette
Design: John van der Woude

Library and Archives Canada Cataloguing in Publication

Boileau, John
Halifax and Titanic / John Boileau.

ISBN 978-1-55109-895-1

1. Halifax (N.S.)—History. 2. Titanic (Steamship). 3. Shipwrecks—North Atlantic Ocean. 4. Disaster victims—North Atlantic Ocean. 5. Cemeteries—Nova Scotia—Halifax. I. Title.

FC2346.4.B65 2012   971.6'22504   C2011-907629-2

Nimbus Publishing acknowledges the financial support for its publishing activities from the Government of Canada through the Canada Book Fund (CBF) and the Canada Council for the Arts, and from the Province of Nova Scotia through the Department of Communities, Culture and Heritage.

For my youngest granddaughter, Zoë, who became fascinated with the *Titanic* story and drew her first pictures of the ship when she was five years old.

CONTENTS

ACKNOWLEDGEMENTS

THE *TITANIC* STORY HAS BEEN TOLD so many times before that it is difficult, but not impossible, to add new information to the tale of the doomed liner. Despite the vast amount of information available, not all of it can be taken at face value. Much of what has been written about *Titanic* is based upon early newspaper reports or the first-hand accounts of survivors. For most survivors, their recollections were limited to their small part in the drama, contained little of the overall picture, and were frequently vague at best. As for newspapers, several journalists simply made up their stories in the absence of facts. There is, however, an enormous amount of trusted literature available on *Titanic*, including the incomparable website Encyclopedia Titanica. Additionally, I am indebted to local authors Alan Ruffman and Blair Beed for their excellent contributions to the story of Halifax's part in the disaster, as well as to Alan Hustak for his painstaking research into Canadians aboard *Titanic*.

For their valuable assistance, thanks are due to two Halifax institutions that hold a vast repository of *Titanic* material: the Nova Scotia Archives and the Maritime Museum of the Atlantic. At the archives, senior archivist Gary Shutlak was never too busy to answer my many *Titanic* inquiries and get me pointed in the right direction; Anjali Vohra worked wonders with obscure images, and several other members of the archives's knowledgeable staff were their usual helpful selves. At the museum, curator Dan Conlin and assistant curator Lynn-Marie

Richard provided prompt assistance with my image research. Additionally, the staff at my publisher, Nimbus, were great to work with once again. Managing editor Patrick Murphy is the very model of what an author looks for in an editor, while production manager Heather Bryan and designer John van der Woude did a first rate job in sorting out my images and text.

As always, thanks to Miriam.

JBB
"Lindisfarne"
Glen Margaret, Nova Scotia

January 18, 2012
200th anniversary of the completion of the paddle steamer Comet, *the first steam vessel to successfully run commercially in Europe.*

A view of Halifax from George's Island about 1890. Halifax Harbour is the second largest anchorage in the world and Canada's main east coast port.

INTRODUCTION

THE FATAL FIRST AND SOLITARY VOYAGE of the Royal Mail Steamer *Titanic* is indelibly inscribed in popular culture. Her tragic sinking, the most famous sea disaster of all time, quickly became part of the public imagination. It has remained there ever since, immortalized in a steady stream of newspaper stories, magazine articles, books, movies, musicals, and websites. There are even groups devoted to *Titanic* research. According to American author Daniel Allen Butler, "It has been said that '*Titanic*' is the third most widely recognized word in the world, following 'God' and 'Coca-cola.'" Whether this is true or not, one hundred years after the tragedy of April 15, 1912, *Titanic*'s sinking continues to fascinate us in a way that few other events do.

The world was shocked to learn of the Titanic disaster; many thought the massive new liner was unsinkable.

Barrington Street in 1902, photographed looking south from George Street. It was Halifax's main commercial area at the time.

At the time, *Titanic* was the world's largest and most luxurious ocean liner. She went to the bottom of the North Atlantic less than three hours after she struck an iceberg on her maiden voyage to New York from Southampton, England, after having called at Cherbourg, France, and Queenston, Ireland. When *Titanic* sank, it was only thirteen days after she had finished her sea trials and five days into her first trip. Among her first-class passengers were some of the wealthiest men and women in the world, old hands at crossing the Atlantic in unparalleled luxury. Several of her second-class passengers, while not millionaires, were certainly very well off. Even among the third-class passengers—also known as steerage—there were many who led a comfortable existence, although by far the vast majority of them were poor emigrants seeking a new life in the United States or Canada. Altogether, there were people from forty-four countries aboard *Titanic*.

A series of seemingly unconnected events—some of them quite minor, but all of them errors or omissions—caused *Titanic* to first strike an iceberg, and then to sink as a result of that collision. A slight change or modification in any one of these incidents could easily have produced completely different outcomes—and saved hundreds of lives. But that is not what happened, and that is one reason why *Titanic*'s story continues to resonate with so many people today.

After *Titanic* sank, Halifax, the capital of Nova Scotia, became intimately involved in the operation mounted to recover as many of the remains of the ship's victims as possible, with bodies then either buried at sea or returned to Halifax. Eventually, 337 bodies were recovered, the majority of them by ships dispatched from Halifax. Of this total, 128 were buried at sea and 209 were delivered to Halifax. The remains of 59 of these victims were sent for burial in their hometowns, while 150 were buried in three Halifax cemeteries. They remain there to this day, the largest number of *Titanic* graves in the world, cared for in perpetuity by the city and visited by thousands of people each year. It is impossible to visit these graves without being moved by the tragic stories surrounding them.

In addition to the three cemeteries, several other sites in Halifax are associated with the *Titanic* tragedy: the waterfront where the remains were delivered, the sites of the morgue and funeral home, the churches where funeral services were conducted, and the homes of the two Haligonians aboard the ship. As well, the Nova Scotia Archives contain a wealth of *Titanic* documents, including the original descriptions of the bodies and their effects, while the Maritime Museum of the Atlantic has one of the most impressive collections of *Titanic* artifacts anywhere in the world. In preserving the memory of *Titanic* and her victims during the last one hundred years, Halifax has undoubtedly lived up to the appellation ascribed to her by famous British author Rudyard Kipling. In his poem *The Song of the Cities*, he bestowed on Halifax the title "Warden of the Honour of the North."

An artist's interpretation of Samuel Cunard standing on the Dartmouth side of Halifax Harbour, while Britannia *steams by.*

CHAPTER 1

UNDER THE WHITE STAR

THE AGE OF STEAM

IT ALL BEGAN WITH SAMUEL CUNARD. The Halifax businessman and entrepreneur took advantage of the sailing ship/steam engine combination to revolutionize the shipping industry. In the early nineteenth century, engineers in Britain, Europe, and North America simultaneously linked a stationary labour-saving device—the steam engine—to a mechanism that drove on its own special tracks—the railway train. Shortly afterwards, the steam engine was adapted for ocean-going vessels and the steamship was born.

Cunard did not invent or improve the steam engine. He was not the first to install a steam engine in a sailing ship, nor were his steamships the first to cross the Atlantic. But he was the first to take advantage of the great paradigm shift that the steamship heralded in both transportation and communications by expanding the Age of Steam to the North Atlantic. Cunard's genius was to establish the first regular transatlantic steamship line. Previously, ships waited dockside until they were either filled with cargo or passengers or a combination of both before they sailed. Cunard began a steamship service with advertised and standardized sailing times, the marine equivalent of a railroad timetable. He even referred to his scheme as an "ocean railway."

An 1849 portrait of Halifax-born entrepreneur Samuel Cunard, who revolutionized transatlantic travel by establishing regular steamship sailings.

Once his flagship, the 1,150-ton *Britannia*, arrived in Halifax from Liverpool, England, on July 16, 1840, after her maiden twelve-and-a-half-day voyage, transatlantic crossings were never the same. Using *Britannia* and three other ships, Cunard established the British and North American Royal Mail Steam Packet Company, which was usually shortened to the Cunard Line. For a decade, the North Atlantic was virtually the sole domain of Cunard. Even when competition eventually arose, his ships remained pre-eminent for many years. One reason that Cunard retained his position was due to his insistence on safety. His ships were neither flashy nor fast, but they were safe. While the ships of other lines experienced dreadful disasters, several of which claimed hundreds of lives, Cunard could continue to boast that his vessels never lost a passenger. Eventually, one shipping company emerged as Cunard's main competitor: the White Star Line.

THE WHITE STAR LINE

IN 1868, THOMAS ISMAY, a director of Britain's National Line, purchased the house flag, trade name, and goodwill of a bankrupt steamship company—the White Star Line—for £1,000. He established a partnership with the world's largest shipyard, Belfast's Harland and Wolff, to build his ships on an unusual (at least for the time) cost-plus basis: the cost of construction plus a fixed percentage of that cost for the builder's profit, providing the shipbuilder would not construct any vessels for rival lines. In 1870, Liverpool shipowner William Imrie joined Ismay and together they formed the Oceanic Steam Navigation Company (the official name of the White Star Line) to operate the ships then under construction.

The new line started with six ships of the Oceanic class and began to operate on the Liverpool to New York run in 1871. Two years later, it suffered a major loss of life when the ss *Atlantic* ran aground at Prospect, near Halifax, due to navigational errors by her crew. A British Board of Trade investigation cleared the company of any wrongdoing and the White Star Line went on to build and operate many famous ships. Five of them captured the Blue Riband, an unofficial

The sinking of the White Star Line's ss Atlantic *off the coast of Nova Scotia in 1873 was the worst transatlantic marine disaster of the nineteenth century.*

accolade awarded to the passenger liner in regular service that made the fastest Atlantic crossing.

THE INTERNATIONAL MERCANTILE MARINE COMPANY

LATE IN THE NINETEENTH CENTURY, shipbuilders began to realize that when speed through water increased above twenty knots, the additional horsepower required to achieve these higher speeds increased logarithmically—that is, each increment in speed required a larger increase in engine power and related coal consumption. This led the White Star Line to concentrate on comfort and reliability, rather than speed. Thomas Ismay died in 1899, and chairmanship of the line passed to his son, J. Bruce Ismay. In 1902, in the face of a rate war with American millionaire J. P. Morgan's newly formed International Mercantile Marine Company (IMM), Ismay agreed to sell the White Star Line to IMM. Two years later, Ismay became chairman of IMM, with the White Star Line as one of the conglomerate's subsidiaries.

Joseph Bruce Ismay was chairman of the White Star Line founded by his father and one of the men who conceived the ships of the Olympic class.

Although there was money to be made in carrying first- and second-class passengers, in the late nineteenth and early twentieth centuries the bread and butter of many steamship lines was the emigrant trade. During this period, millions of people from Europe were transported to the United States and Canada, as well as further afield to countries such as Australia. The White Star Line quickly established a niche market for itself in carrying emigrants. It was among the first to offer modestly priced third-class accommodation along with more expensive first- and second-class accommodation in the same ship. Even then, its third-class areas were comparable to higher classes on many other lines and boasted such luxuries as dining rooms with linen-covered tables and silverware. White Star ships were built to carry larger numbers of third-class passengers than other lines and advertised extensively throughout Europe for emigrants. In a clever marketing ploy, menus were printed on the back of postcards, which emigrants could then mail home to tell their friends and families the benefits of sailing on the White Star Line.

Meanwhile, *Lusitania* and *Mauretania*, ships of White Star's main rival, Cunard, had entered service in 1907 and were widely regarded as superior to anything else then crossing the North Atlantic. Later that year, Ismay met with the chairman of Harland and Wolff, Lord Pirrie (who was also a director of the White Star Line), to discuss White Star's response to Cunard's latest challenge. William Pirrie had been born in Quebec City in 1847 of Irish parents, was taken to Ireland when he was two years old, and spent the rest of his life there. He began working for Harland and Wolff in 1862 as a gentleman apprentice and rose steadily to the top, serving as chairman from 1895 until his death in 1924.

OLYMPIC CLASS

IN 1907, DURING AFTER-DINNER drinks, Pirrie and Ismay discussed ideas for a new class of three large, luxury liners, to be called the Olympic class, which would appeal to the wealthy, as well as to the growing and increasingly prosperous middle class. Even third-class passengers would be treated like second-class travellers on the ships of other lines. The ships would be larger than any vessels previously constructed. In keeping with the sense of grandeur the ships were meant to purvey, they would be named *Olympic*, *Titanic*, and *Gigantic* (later renamed *Britannic*). Design of the new class was initially the responsibility of Alexander Carlisle (Pirrie's brother-in-law), head designer at Harland and Wolff until he retired in 1910, when his replacement Thomas Andrews (Pirrie's nephew) took over. Ismay and Pirrie also contributed their ideas to the design.

To build *Olympic*, the lead ship of the class, Harland and Wolff upgraded their Belfast facilities, including combining three slipways into two larger ones to accommodate the vast size of the new class. To ease pressure on the shipyard, *Titanic*'s construction started three months after *Olympic*'s began. *Olympic* was launched on October 20, 1910, and made her maiden voyage on June 14, 1911. She went on to a long and illustrious career, which lasted from 1911 to 1935. On September 20, 1911, *Olympic* collided with the British battleship HMS *Hawke*

The White Star Line's ss Olympic was Titanic's sister ship. In 1919 she carried Nova Scotia's 25th Battalion from Europe to Halifax after the First World War.

off the Isle of Wight, flooding two compartments and twisting her propeller shaft. The Royal Navy blamed *Olympic* for the incident, claiming that her huge displacement had created suction that pulled *Hawke* into her side. *Olympic's* captain at the time was Edward Smith, who very shortly would be appointed to command *Titanic*.

During the First World War, *Olympic* was used as a fast troop transport. In 1917 and 1918, the Canadian government chartered her to carry soldiers to Britain, while after the war she brought many Canadian soldiers home. On one occasion in 1918, while transporting American troops to Europe, *Olympic* sighted, rammed, and sank the German submarine *U-103*. It is the only known instance of a merchant vessel sinking an enemy warship during the entire war. *Olympic's* remarkable wartime record earned her the epithet "Old Reliable."

BUILDING *TITANIC*

CONSTRUCTION OF *TITANIC* BEGAN on March 31, 1909, but was twice delayed due to repairs to *Olympic*. The first instance occurred when Harland and Wolff had to use *Titanic's* propeller shaft to replace the one damaged in the *Hawke* incident. Then *Olympic* lost a propeller blade and shipyard men and materiel being used for *Titanic* had to be diverted to *Olympic* to effect repairs. Eventually,

Titanic *slides from her construction gantry in Belfast on May 31, 1911. It took ten more months to complete her fitting out.*

it took more than three thousand men working for three years to build *Titanic*, at a cost of £1.5 million.

Once *Titanic's* hull was launched on May 31, 1911, her fitting out commenced and was completed on March 31, 1912. During that time, the empty shell of the hull became the most luxurious vessel afloat and consisted of seven passenger decks, starting with A at the top down to G at the bottom. The ship's safety was to be ensured by a double bottom or hull and several watertight compartments. The double bottom consisted of a series of forty-four sealed tanks, which were two metres high and filled with water ballast. In the event of a grounding or collision, the outer hull might be breached, but the inner one would remain intact and prevent flooding or sinking. Although the hull along the bottom was double, this did not extend up the sides of the ship. In addition, the lower hull was divided into sixteen watertight compartments by fifteen lateral bulkheads that ran from one side of *Titanic* to the other and from the top of the double bottom to either D or E Deck. These were designed so that *Titanic* could stay afloat if any two large amidship compartments or the first four forward ones flooded. In addition, large electrically and manually controlled doors between the bulkheads could be shut in an instant if flooding started. A unique float device also closed the doors automatically if more than fifteen centimetres of water entered any compartment.

Titanic was a massive vessel. At the time she was built, *Titanic* was the largest human-made, moveable object in history, with an overall length of 269 metres

---

CONSTRUCTION MYTHS

At least two myths about the building of *Titanic* persist to this day. The first one claims that a shipyard workman was accidentally trapped inside the ship's double bottom during her construction, supposedly because of the speed with which work on the giant ship proceeded. As proof, it is claimed that several shipyard workers and even some passengers heard hammering from inside the hull. In hindsight, it is easy to see how such a myth may have started. At the end of each shift, supervisors checked the work completed during that shift. In the time-honoured method of checking rivets, they tapped on the rivet head to ensure tightness. Perhaps older workers teased the newer ones with tall tales of workmen trapped inside hulls.

The story of the trapped worker may also have originated with British engineering genius Isambard Kingdom Brunel's massive ship, *Great Eastern,* launched in 1860. After an unsuccessful career as a passenger ship and cable ship, she was broken up for scrap in 1888. When workers took her apart, they reportedly found a worker's skeleton inside the vessel's double bottom.

The second *Titanic* construction myth began to circulate shortly after the disaster and concerned the ship's alleged hull number, 390904. When held up to a mirror, the reversed image of the number reads "NO POPE." As a result, thousands of primarily Catholic workers prepared to walk off the job, bringing construction to a halt. According to the story, management assured the workers that this was just a coincidence, and the work continued. In fact, *Titanic*'s shipyard-assigned hull number was 401, while her Board of Trade registration number was 131,428. At no time was the number 390904 ever associated with *Titanic*. Additionally, the workforce was overwhelmingly Protestant, and such an incident would not have bothered them.

Titanic's *Café Parisien on the starboard side of B deck became a popular place for some of the ship's younger first-class adult passengers to congregate.*

and a beam of 28 metres. From the waterline to the boat deck (immediately above A deck) she was 18 metres high, while the distance from her keel to the top of her funnels was 53 metres. *Titanic* had a gross weight of 46,328 tons and a displacement of 66,000 tons. Her service speed was 21 knots and she had a top speed of 24 knots. To attain this speed, 29 coal-fired boilers provided steam to her two engines—still the largest ever built. Fully loaded, she could carry 3,547 passengers and crew.

SEA TRIALS

ON APRIL 2, AFTER A DAY'S delay due to weather, *Titanic* underwent trials in the Irish Sea to certify her seaworthiness. Testing consisted of various manoeuvres, which included steaming at 20 knots, drifting to a stop after the engines had stopped, turning with rudder only and propellers only, start-stop tests, and a wheel hard-over turn. The final major task was a stopping test from full speed, with the engines put full astern. It took about 775 metres for *Titanic* to come to a halt. *Titanic* then cruised on a straight course for about two hours before she turned and headed back for Belfast. On the way, she performed several sharp port and starboard turns to check her handling. Near Belfast, one final test was completed: the lowering of the port and starboard anchors. Once this was done, Francis Carruthers, the Board of Trade surveyor, signed "An Agreement and Account of Voyages and Crew," valid for a period of twelve months. The monster ship was now certified by the British Board of Trade to carry passengers. After dropping off all non-crew members to be ferried ashore at about

8:00 P.M., *Titanic* turned and steamed towards Southampton, 965 kilometres distant, to take on coal, provisions, additional crew members, and passengers for her maiden voyage, a mere week away.

TITANIC'S DEPARTMENTS

TITANIC'S CREW WAS DIVIDED into various departments, each with varying responsibilities towards the ship or its passengers. The deck department consisted of the ship's eight officers and two surgeons, plus quartermasters, masters-at-arms, boatswains, lookouts, officers' stewards, various tradesmen, and several able bodied seamen. This was to be the last voyage for *Titanic's* captain, Edward John Smith, after which he intended to retire. When Canadian passenger Major Arthur Peuchen, aware of Smith's accident with *Olympic*, learned Smith would command *Titanic*, he proclaimed, "Surely we're not going to have that man."

Titanic's officers besides Captain Smith consisted of Chief Officer Henry Wilde, First Officer William Murdoch, Second Officer Charles Lightoller, Third Officer Herbert Pitman, Fourth Officer Joseph Boxhall, Fifth Officer Harold Lowe, and

Sixth Officer James Moody. Wilde had been drafted from *Olympic* by Smith, who decided at the last minute that he needed another officer familiar with the large Olympic class. This transfer bumped the top two remaining officers down a position. It also caused original Second Officer David Blair to leave the ship. When he departed, he inadvertently took the keys to a storage locker in his cabin where the binoculars for the lookouts in the crow's nest were kept, with unfortunate results. Generally, the officers were an experienced and able group of men.

The other departments on *Titanic* were the engineering department (325 engineers, boilermen, firemen/

Captain Edward John Smith had been at sea since he was seventeen and was the White Star Line's senior captain.

TITANIC IN FILM

The 1958 British film *A Night to Remember*, based on American author Walter Lord's classic account of the same name, is commonly regarded as the most accurate portrayal of the *Titanic* disaster. In the film's opening scene, a woman is shown on a flag-bedecked platform, flanked by J. Bruce Ismay and Thomas Andrews, along with several other dignitaries. In a cradle in front of the woman, a bottle of champagne rests horizontally, secured at top and bottom by cords. As she makes the traditional christening statement ("I name this ship *Titanic*. May God bless her and all who sail in her"), she releases the bottle, which swings forward and smashes open against the hull.

Despite the film's reputation for accuracy, the scene is a complete fabrication; the White Star Line's standard policy was never to christen its ships. (Ironically, the fact that *Titanic* was not christened caused many people to claim that the ship was cursed and this was the reason she foundered.) In reality, the movie footage of the event shows the launching of *Queen Elizabeth* in 1938. The film also contains an error in *Titanic*'s configuration as it incorrectly shows smoke coming from all four funnels. Although the ship was fitted with four funnels, only the three forward ones were real; the fourth one was a dummy. Its purpose was to improve the ship's lines and appearance. But it did have a practical purpose, as it provided ventilation for the turbine and reciprocating engine rooms.

---

stokers, trimmers, greasers, and electricians) under Chief Engineer Joseph Bell, and the victualling department (417 stewards—21 of them women—plus kitchen and galley staff) under Chief Purser Hugh McElroy. Several miscellaneous groups that technically were not crew members but are normally included in crew totals were also part of the ship's crew. This included 68 à la carte restaurant staff, drawn from the two London restaurants of manager Luigi Gatti (who paid them wages in addition to a small salary provided by the line), 9 members of the Harland and Wolff guarantee group headed by Thomas Andrews, 8 musicians led by bandmaster Wallace Hartley, 5 postal clerks (two British, three American), and 2 Marconi operators—Harold Bride and Jack Phillips.

SOUTHAMPTON

BY 8:00 A.M. ON April 10, 1912, the remainder of *Titanic*'s crew members had arrived and set about their jobs of making final preparations for the arrival of passengers. Captain Maurice Clarke of the Board of Trade came aboard to oversee the crew muster, witness each crew member signing the ship's articles, and then sign off on them himself as each of the ship's departments was completed. Several crewmen who had signed on earlier did not show up and were immediately replaced by substitutes on hand for just this occurrence. Clarke then ordered the manning and lowering of two lifeboats. Starboard Lifeboats 11 and 15 were lowered to the water, each with a crew of eight. They rowed around the ship to the dock and back again before being hoisted to the davits on the boat deck.

At 9:30, Ismay, who was going to New York to attend a meeting of the IMM, came aboard and occupied a lavish three-room promenade suite on B deck, specifically designed for J. P. Morgan's use. (Morgan was unable to make the maiden voyage due to an influenza-type illness.) At the same time, with formalities over, most of the crew were released to their duties, depending on the watch to which they were assigned. Members of the eight o'clock to twelve o'clock watch went to their work areas, members of the twelve o'clock to four o'clock watch were put on standby, while those in the four o'clock to eight o'clock watch could do what they wanted. For some members of the latter watch, this meant a trip ashore and a pint or two in a nearby pub. Substitutes not already accepted also remained on the ship to replace anyone who might not return from their brief run ashore. Now all that was needed before the massive ship could sail on her maiden transatlantic voyage were passengers and coal.

Titanic *departs Southampton on Wednesday, April 10, 1912.*

CHAPTER 2

TITANIC SAILS

THE EDWARDIAN AGE

ALTHOUGH EDWARD VII DIED IN 1910 after a short nine-year reign, he had indelibly stamped his brief era with the term "Edwardian." For some historians, the Edwardian period even extends after his death until 1912 (*Titanic* disaster), 1914 (start of the First World War), 1918 (end of the First World War), or as late as 1919 (Treaty of Versailles). Throughout her long reign, Edward's mother, Victoria, had placed a strong emphasis on morality and family values following the sexual, financial, and personal scandals of previous members of the House of Hanover that preceded her reign.

By contrast, Edward personified the leisured, fashionable elite that was fond of travel and was influenced by the art and fashions of continental Europe. By the time he became king at age fifty-nine, he had already established a reputation as a playboy, gambler, and ladies' man who entertained on a lavish scale. Although society was controlled by a rigid class system at the time, cracks were beginning to appear, hastened by the rise of socialism, concern over the plight of the poor, rapid industrialization, and women's suffrage. To the upper classes, much of this was invisible and they carried on with their interests in leisure activities and the arts. The era was later popularized as a romantic golden age of languid summer afternoons and indolent garden parties.

It was also an era of tremendous technological change, which saw the first advantages of modern industrialization and mass production. In both Britain and the United States, slightly more than 1 percent of the population controlled 66 percent of the wealth. The comings and goings of this group of people were followed by the masses, much as the careers of actors, musicians, or sports personalities are now. Yet, for the very wealthy, there were not as many opportunities for conspicuous consumption as there are today. The excesses of private jets, flashy cars, and elite holiday hideaways so preferred by the nouveau riche were still in the future. While ownership of several fine homes in various locations containing expensive *objets d'art* provided one opportunity for ostentatious displays of wealth, transatlantic crossings on luxury liners—especially a maiden voyage—were another method favoured by many of the upper class. And sailing on the maiden voyage of the greatest, most luxurious ship the world had ever seen—which one British newspaper labelled "a twentieth century marvel afloat"—held the greatest cachet of all.

THE COAL STRIKE

IN EARLY 1912, British coal miners went on strike in an attempt to replace a very complicated wage structure with the concept of a minimum wage for all men and boys working in the mines. The strike affected trains, ships, factories, and ordinary households alike and was still in effect when *Titanic* docked at Southampton. As a result, several White Star Line ships (as well as those of other lines) were stranded in port. Coal was taken from the company's other ships, transferred to *Titanic*, and added to what remained from Belfast. With these measures, the ship had enough coal to make the trip to New York, where coal for the return voyage would be obtained. To conserve fuel, *Titanic* would steam at an average speed of twenty-two knots, less than her top speed. Because of the coal strike, many passengers who had booked on other vessels either transferred to *Titanic* or were reassigned to her by the White Star Line.

Titanic would normally carry 8,000 tons of coal, enough for one return transatlantic crossing. While firemen or stokers fed coal by hand into 159 furnaces, trimmers worked continuously to supply it to the firemen and keep it spread evenly to maintain a balanced load inside the bunkers. At sea, the furnaces consumed 650 tons of coal a day—more than 4 tons per furnace, all shovelled by hand. In *Titanic*'s case, a bit more coal than normal was being consumed as a spontaneous combustion fire had been smouldering since taking on coal in Belfast. The fire was in the bottom of the coalbunker in boiler room No. 5, beside the watertight bulkhead shared with boiler room No. 6. In itself this was not an unusual incident in the age of coal-powered ships and stokers were fighting it the standard way—in this case shovelling away about a thousand tons of coal to get to the fire. Although several key people were aware of the fire, including the captain, the chief engineer, and the ship's designer, it was not reported to the Board of Trade inspector.

FIRST-CLASS FACILITIES

THE PUBLIC ROOMS FOR first-class passengers on *Titanic* included the dining saloon, reception room, lounge, reading and writing room, smoking room, verandah and palm court cafés, and an à la carte restaurant. The latter establishment was a new experiment, as passengers paid for anything consumed there on an individual basis, rather than being included in the price of their tickets. They could also arrange private parties in the restaurant. Among the unusual first-class amenities for the time were a gymnasium, swimming pool (the first ever on a ship), Turkish and electric saunas, squash court, and three elevators (out of six on the ship). Other features were a barber shop, photography darkroom, pressing room for clothes, library, and in-room telephones.

First-class common areas were opulent and stunningly decorated with the most expensive materials available, such as mahogany, marble, leather, and silk. The eye-catching centrepiece in first class was the elaborate Grand Staircase, which swept down four decks from a glass and wrought-iron dome above A Deck through to the first-class entrance on D Deck, immediately in front of the first-class dining saloon. This facility could seat 532 people and was the largest room on any ship afloat at the time.

Accommodation for first class contained full-sized beds, rather than berths, and had washstands with hot and cold running water. The rooms were decorated in a variety of styles and ranged from single staterooms to suites of three, four, or five rooms. The most luxurious were the two promenade suites on B Deck, among the most expensive shipboard accommodation ever.

Many first-class passengers always travelled with their maids, servants, and valets, who were regarded as indispensible assistants and, in many cases, confidants. There were thirty-one of them aboard *Titanic* and the White Star Line took great care to treat them properly. While they clearly were not first-class passengers, they were not ordinary working class people either. The solution was a separate dining room and promenade for their exclusive use.

FIRST-CLASS PASSENGERS

AT 11:30 ON APRIL 10, 1912, the train from London's Waterloo Station carrying most of the 193 first-class passengers arrived at the White Star Line's dock in Southampton. Although it was only thirty minutes before *Titanic*'s scheduled departure, these passengers were met by the chief steward and individually escorted to their cabins by stewards. The extensive publicity surrounding *Titanic*'s maiden voyage had convinced many of the rich and famous of the day to sail on her, including several leaders in business, politics, culture, and other fields.

Isidor Straus had been born in Germany and immigrated to the United States with his family in 1854 when he was nine years old. The family settled initially in Georgia, where Isidor began working as a clerk in his father's store. During the American Civil War (1861–1865), he worked for a company engaged in the dangerous job of blockade-running for the Confederacy. After the war, the family moved to New York, where Isidor and a brother obtained a license to sell their family china and glassware in the R. H. Macy and Company department store. In 1895, they acquired joint ownership of Macy's. Although Isidor and his wife, Ida, normally sailed on German liners, this time they decided to travel on *Titanic*. Travelling with them were Isidor's manservant, John Farthing, and Ida's maid, Ellen Bird. The Strauses' net worth was estimated at $50 million.

Major Archibald Butt was a close personal friend of U.S. President William Taft and later became his aide-de-camp. He had also been aide-de-camp to President Theodore Roosevelt and tried—unsuccessfully—to remain neutral during the acrimonious squabbles between the two Republicans. Exhausted by their quarrels, he travelled to Europe for a rest, in the company of another close friend: artist, sculptor, and author Francis David Millet. The two were returning to Washington, DC, together.

Another military man aboard *Titanic* was Colonel Archibald Gracie, the son of a Confederate general killed during the Civil War. One of his ancestors had built Gracie Mansion, the official residence of the mayor of New York City. Gracie had spent the previous several years writing a book about the Battle of Chickamauga, in which his father fought. With the book published, he had taken a trip to Europe to relax and was returning home.

Famous American fiction writer Jacques Futrelle and his wife, Lily May, were returning to Massachusetts. Some people believe that Futrelle's books were the inspiration for Agatha Christie's novels. William Thomas Stead was another famous author and journalist; he was on his way to New York to speak at a peace congress. Ironically, he had written two fictional stories that foreshadowed *Titanic*'s fate. In 1886 he wrote "How the Mail Steamer Went Down in Mid-Atlantic, by a Survivor," in which a ship collides with another, causing a large loss of life due to an insufficient number of lifeboats. Then, in 1892, he wrote "From

LEFT *Isidor Straus owned New York's most famous department store, Macy's.*
RIGHT *American author William Thomas Stead had written two stories that were eerily similar to* Titanic's *fate.*

Philadelphian John Thayer had been on a European holiday with his wife, Marian, and their son, Jack.

the Old World to the New," about a ship that hits an iceberg and whose survivors are saved by the White Star vessel *Majestic*. While Stead got to live out his stories, he did not survive to describe this one.

Millionaire banker George Widener of Philadelphia was returning from a European vacation with his wife, Eleanor, twenty-seven-year-old son, Harry—a collector of rare books—and two servants, valet Edwin Keeping and maid Amalie Gieger. George's father was the richest man in Philadelphia and a board member of the parent company that controlled IMM. Another wealthy Philadelphia family was the Thayers. John Thayer, second vice-president of the Pennsylvania Railroad, was returning from a visit to Europe with his wife, Marian, one of their four children, seventeen-year-old Jack, and Marian's maid, Margaret Fleming.

SECOND-CLASS FACILITIES

MUCH OF THE LAVISHNESS and attention to detail in first-class areas continued into second class. Both public and private second-class rooms were on a par with first-class ones on other lines. Second-class had its own elevator and grand staircase, although the latter was smaller than the one in first class. Perhaps the best feature available to second-class passengers was the dining arrangements: a shared galley with first class, certainly one of the finest anywhere in the world.

SECOND-CLASS PASSENGERS

SECOND- AND THIRD-class passengers travelling from London had arrived on the same train at 9:30 and began to board immediately. Among the 234 second-class passengers was the only Japanese aboard, Masabumi

The ministrations of Father Thomas Byles would later offer solace to many people in their last minutes.

Hosono, a Tokyo civil servant, while London science teacher Lawrence Beesley was on his way to make a long tour around America. He thought that he would have to wait until New York to get a full view of *Titanic*, as the narrow approach to the dock made this impossible at Southampton. Catholic priest Father Thomas Byles was headed for New York to officiate at the wedding of his brother, while Nellie Becker was en route to Michigan from India with her three young children Ruth, Marion, and Richard. Her missionary husband had stayed behind while Nellie travelled to the United States for treatment of a disease her one-year-old son had contracted.

THIRD-CLASS FACILITIES

ALTHOUGH PASSENGERS IN third class did not have access to many of the amenities provided for first-class passengers, their accommodation and meal arrangements surpassed anything else then available on the ships of other lines. Berths for third class were split between the forward and after sections of *Titanic*, with married couples and single men near the bow and families and single women in the stern. Uniquely, the White Star Line did not allow single men and women travelling third class to be berthed near each other. Although not decorated to the standards of the other classes of cabins, third-class rooms were large, clean, and comfortable.

While food for third-class passengers was plain, it was tasty and plentiful. For many, especially those from impoverished backgrounds, this was a real luxury. Third-class dining facilities were conveniently located amidships, handy for those berthed either forward or aft. A large common area in the stern was provided as a general-purpose room for third class, and dances and singing took place there every night. A strange oversight was the lack of bathing facilities; there were only two bathtubs available for all of third class, more than seven hundred passengers on this voyage. Additionally, both bathtubs were in the stern, a long journey for those accommodated forward.

THIRD-CLASS PASSENGERS

THIRD CLASS WAS often known as "steerage," from the time when cheap accommodation was located at the stern, where a ship's steering gear was situated. At Southampton, 497 steerage passengers boarded, and of the 134 British passengers, two families alone accounted for 19 of them. John and Annie Sage were on their way from Peterborough, England, to Florida with their nine children, ages four to twenty, while Fred and Augusta Goodwin, along with their six children, ages one to sixteen, were moving to New York state from Wiltshire. A smaller British family was the Deans of Hampshire. Bertram, Ettie, and two infants, twenty-month-old Bert and nine-week-old Millvina were on their way to join family and friends in Wichita, Kansas, where Bertram hoped to open a tobacco shop.

One hundred and thirty Scandinavians were also emigrating to the United States. Among them were two mothers travelling with their children to join their husbands in America. Maria Panula was on her way to Pennsylvania from Finland with her five children, as well as the twenty-three-year-old daughter of a neighbour, who was perhaps along to help with the children. From Sweden, Alma Pålsson was travelling with her four young children to Chicago, where her husband had secured employment.

FIRST-CLASS CANADIAN PASSENGERS

ALTHOUGH SEVERAL CANADIAN passengers were aboard *Titanic* when she sank, most references fail to state this fact. The main reason is that at the time there was no such class of people as "Canadians." It was not until 1947 that "Canadian" legally existed as a distinct nationality; before that Canadians were simply considered British. In addition to those whom we would today consider Canadian citizens, there were also several other passengers headed to Canada. Author Alan Hustak has done the most extensive research about Canadians aboard *Titanic*. In his 1998 book, *Titanic: The Canadian Story*, Hustak states that there were more than 120 men, women, and children bound for Canada, either as returning citizens, emigrants, visitors, or businessmen.

Among the first-class passengers boarding at Southampton was the Allison family of Montreal. "Hud" (short for Hudson) Allison was a self-made million-aire and the junior partner in the brokerage firm of Johnson, McConnell, and Allison, which had been started by his uncle and John McConnell, a future owner of the *Montreal Star*. In Montreal business circles, the trio was known as the "Methodist Mafia." Travelling with him was his American-born wife, Bessie, and

LEFT *"Hud" Allison was returning to Montreal from a British holiday with his wife, two children, and four servants.*
RIGHT *American-born Charles Melville Hays was the president of Canada's Grand Trunk Railway.*

their two children, Loraine, two months shy of her third birthday, and Trevor, only eleven months. The entourage also included four servants hired in England: the children's nanny, Alice Cleaver, maid Sarah Daniels, cook Mildred Brown, and chauffeur George Swane.

The Allisons were very pious and contributed money and labour to their church. Their Methodism did not preclude the family from enjoying the finer things in life, however. During their British trip, Hud had purchased two dozen Clydesdale and Hackney stallions and mares in Scotland. The horses were being shipped separately on another vessel and were intended for the new stock farm he operated with his brother just south of Ottawa near Winchester. Hud and his wife also bought furniture for their house in Winchester and their new one in Montreal's prestigious Westmount. To accommodate the family, nanny, and maid, Hud had booked three staterooms on the upper deck, as well as second-class accommodation for the cook and chauffer. He had even changed the family's original travel plans so they could sail on *Titanic* with some old friends. The Allison family's fate would be one of the most tragic on a voyage earmarked by tragedy.

Another prominent Canadian family was the Fortunes of Winnipeg. Mark Fortune had made his money buying up Métis land after the failed Riel Rebellion of 1870. After the defeated Métis left Winnipeg to head further west in attempt to get away from the restrictive rules of the white man and establish their own government, Fortune bought a thousand acres along the Assiniboine River. When Portage Avenue, Winnipeg's main street, was surveyed through his property a few years later, he became a rich man.

Mark had decided to treat his wife, Mary, and the four of his six children still at home (the two eldest were living on their own in British Columbia) to the "Grand Tour," a popular and long-standing tradition established by young, upper-class British men. The Grand Tour was viewed as an educational rite of passage and conformed to a standard European itinerary that included many of the continent's major cities. From the second half of the eighteenth century, wealthy American and Canadian youth joined in, to be followed by members of the middle class once rail and steamship travel made the journey less of a burden. The British firm of Thomas Cook capitalized on this tradition, and "Cook's Tour" became a byword for a guided but cursory tour of the major attractions of a certain area.

The Fortune children on the trip were Ethel, twenty-eight, Alice, twenty-four, Mabel, twenty-three, and Charles, nineteen. Although Ethel's engagement to

Crawford Gordon, a Toronto banker, had already been announced, she agreed to postpone her wedding so that she could help chaperone her younger siblings and purchase her trousseau in Europe. Her younger sister, Mabel, had also fallen in love, but with a Minnesotan jazz musician of whom her parents did not approve. They hoped that an extended trip abroad might end that romance. The youngest of the Fortune girls, Alice, was also engaged. Her fiancé was Charles Allen, a businessman from New Brunswick. Charles Fortune, the youngest member of the family, was the main reason for the trip. He had recently graduated from Bishop's College School in Lennoxville, Quebec, an event his father had waited for before taking the family on the Grand Tour.

Travelling with the Fortune family were three prosperous bachelors: realtor Thomson Beattie and stock broker Hugo Ross from Winnipeg, plus bank president Thomas McCaffry from Vancouver. They had left Winnipeg with the Fortunes on January 8, 1912, travelled by train to New York, sailed on the Cunard liner *Franconia* to Trieste (via Algiers, Monaco, and Athens), and then journeyed by rail through Greece before sailing on to the Holy Land and Egypt. The party returned via Venice, Paris, and London. In Paris, exhausted by their travels, they cancelled later plans to sail home on the Cunarder *Mauretania*, the fastest liner afloat, and booked passage on *Titanic*'s maiden voyage. When it came time to board at Southampton, Ross was so ill with dysentery that he had to be carried aboard on a stretcher.

American-born Charles Melville Hays had worked for various railroads in the United States since he was a teenager. In 1896, he moved to Montreal as general manager of the Grand Trunk Railway and became its president in 1910. He convinced the government to back a second transcontinental line (which later became the Canadian National Railway) to compete with the Canadian Pacific Railway. Hayes was in England trying to resolve debt problems with the new company's British board of directors. His solution might sound familiar today: he proposed to spend the company's way out of financial difficulty.

Hays was travelling with his wife, Clara; their daughter and her husband, Orian and Thornton Davidson; the family maid, Anne Perreault; and Hays's private secretary, Vivian Payne—all as guests of Ismay. The group had been enjoying itself in England for a month when word was received that one of the four Hays daughters was having a difficult time in pregnancy, which might require a caesarean section. This, coupled with the opening of the railway's flagship Château Laurier Hotel in Ottawa, convinced Hays to return to Canada. Paul Romaine Chevré, a French sculptor who had sculpted a marble bust of Prime Minister Sir Wilfrid

Laurier for the hotel's lobby, was also a part of Hays's entourage. Chevré was used to transatlantic travel. He spent six months each year at his Quebec City office getting orders for work and the remaining six months in France making the figures.

The richest Canadian aboard *Titanic* was Harry Markland Molson, a fourth-generation member of the famed Montreal brewing, banking, and shipbuilding family. Harry had inherited the brewery and bank in 1897 and used his new-found wealth to enjoy life, so much so that his friends dubbed him Merry Larkwand Molson. A bachelor, Harry was an experienced yachtsman and a strong swimmer. He had already survived two marine disasters: he swam away from a sinking ship in the Gulf of St. Lawrence in 1899 and from another one in the St. Lawrence River in 1904. Despite his fortune, on *Titanic* Molson had a modest inside cabin on the upper deck. Molson had been convinced to return to Canada aboard *Titanic* by his friend, Toronto millionaire Major Arthur Peuchen, president of the Standard Chemical Company. Peuchen was a member of a prestigious Toronto militia regiment and the country's second-oldest infantry unit, the Queen's Own Rifles of Canada. Like Harry Molson, Peuchen was also an expert yachtsman and—despite his wealth—also had an unpretentious inside cabin, even though he was carrying $217,000 worth of stocks and bonds with him.

The one Halifax millionaire aboard was George Wright, who had made his fortune in printing international business directories, an idea that occurred to him during a visit to the American Centennial Exhibition in Philadelphia in 1876. He had other business interests in real estate and construction and on the personal side enjoyed hunting, fishing, and dancing. The very private Wright was a lifelong bachelor and a prude when it came to literature, obscenity, gambling, theatre, and movies. He even wrote letters to the editor of the *New York Times* in 1909 and 1910 decrying increasing profanity, especially among boys. In other areas, he was surprisingly ahead of his time. He believed in the integration of housing for all classes, and built homes for the working poor and middle and upper classes close to each other, with his own impressive mansion nearby. He also supported the emancipation of women. Shortly before his trip, he had amended his will to bequeath his stately home to the Council of Women in Halifax. Despite Wright's imposing presence, he was not seen on deck after *Titanic* hit the iceberg.

Bert and Vera Dick of Calgary had been married the day *Titanic* was launched and were returning from a late honeymoon in the Holy Land and on the Grand

LEFT *Halifax millionaire George Wright was one of only two Haligonians aboard* Titanic.
RIGHT *George Graham was returning from a European buying trip for his employer, the T. Eaton Company in Winnipeg.*

Tour of major European cities via London, where they stopped to purchase reproduction antiques for their new Tudor-style house in Calgary's posh Mount Royal neighbourhood. At thirty-one, Bert was almost twice the age of his seventeen-year-old bride and had made his money as a property developer and building contractor. When *Titanic*'s designer, Thomas Andrews, discovered the date of the Dicks' marriage, he quickly befriended them and spent time with the couple aboard the ship. On one occasion he told them, "I believe this ship to be as nearly perfect as human brains can make her."

George Graham, a buyer for the T. Eaton Company in Winnipeg, was one of several commercial salesmen travelling first class. Originally from St. Mary's, Ontario (between London and Stratford), he had started in retail as a teenager before joining Eaton's in 1903 in Toronto. Graham was transferred to their new Winnipeg store in 1906, the year after he married Edith Jackson, to head up the company's crockery and fine china department. Although he was reluctant to leave his wife alone as she had suffered a miscarriage after the death of their young son, Graham was on a company buying trip to England, Belgium, and Austria. He was originally scheduled to sail on *Mauretania*, but when he discovered that he could get home three days earlier on *Titanic*, he changed his booking.

SECOND-CLASS CANADIAN PASSENGERS

THE HART FAMILY—Benjamin, Esther, and seven-year-old Eva—of Ilford, Essex, was emigrating to Canada. A building contractor in England, Benjamin intended to open a hardware store in Winnipeg. Like so many others, the family had originally booked passage on another ship but, because of the coal strike, were transferred to *Titanic*. Throughout the voyage, Esther was troubled by premonitions that some terrible tragedy would befall them. Years later, Eva recalled that her mother told her father that "she had made up her mind quite firmly that she would not go to bed in that ship, she would sit up at night..." Esther stuck to her guns; she stayed awake each night and slept during the day.

Like the Harts, three Hickman brothers from Hampshire, England, were also emigrating to Canada. Lewis had already spent six years in northern Manitoba and convinced the entire eleven-person Hickman family to join him. Due to the coal strike, however, passage was only obtained for Lewis and two of his brothers, Leonard, and Stanley. Four other young men from their hometown joined them on the voyage. All seven perished.

Léopold Weisz, a Jew originally from Hungary, moved to England, where he met and married Belgian native Mathilde Pëde, a Roman Catholic nine years his senior. Léopold trained as a stone carver in Britain at the Bromsgrove Guild of Art (where Mathilde was also studying) and found work in his trade in Montreal. He returned to England to bring his wife to Canada. They were originally booked to travel first class on another ship, but because of the coal strike were transferred to *Titanic*.

THIRD-CLASS CANADIAN PASSENGERS

MOST OF THE third-class passengers sailing to Canada were not making the journey for pleasure; they were emigrating to begin new lives, mostly in the west. Among them were several Scandinavians. The Andersson family from Sweden—Anders, his wife Alfrida, four girls aged two to eleven, and a boy of four—was emigrating to Winnipeg. Alfrida's sister, Sigrid Danbom, and her husband, Ernest, had persuaded them to move to Canada, having already bought a farm in Iowa. The two families were travelling together, and the Danboms, who also had their four-month-old son with them, intended to visit relatives in Winnipeg before moving on to their new farm. A number of Finns were also emigrating to Canada. Four of them were going to Sudbury, Ontario, including farmer Iisakki Nirva and three younger men. Nirva had sold his farm and left behind his wife and five children to join him later. Farm hands Karl Wiklund and his younger brother, Jacob, were on their way to the Eastern Townships in Quebec. None of these Finns survived; only Jacob's body was found.

Brothers Lewis and Owen Braund from Devonshire, England, were also emigrating to Canada to begin farming in Saskatchewan's Qu'Appelle Valley. They had been encouraged by their older brother, Jim, who had moved to Saskatoon in the early 1900s where he worked on a farm. Travelling with the brothers were four distant male cousins and a female neighbour. Both brothers perished in the sinking. For some unknown reason, even though Jim was in England on a visit, he did not sail on *Titanic*, but returned to Canada on a ship out of Liverpool.

DEPARTURE

EXPERIENCED HARBOUR PILOT George Bowyer boarded *Titanic* at 11:15 and made his way to the bridge where he discussed departure procedures with Captain Smith and the ship's officers. At noon, the ship's whistles blew, the gangway was lowered, and five tugs pulled *Titanic* away from the dock and turned her to face downriver. On the order "ahead slow," the massive vessel began to move, slowly picking up speed. The ship's forward movement, coupled with the low tide, caused a surge of water to flow away from *Titanic*. On one side the water flowed harmlessly into the River Test, but on the other it headed for the docks, where two ships idled by the coal strike were tied up in tandem, *Oceanic* on the inside and *New York* on the outside.

The crest of water initially lifted *New York* as it surged past, then dropped her—bobbing up and down—back to her former level. Within seconds, the strain on *New York*'s mooring ropes snapped the stern ones and *Titanic*'s increasing speed drew both water and *New York* toward her. *New York* came within a metre of colliding, prevented only by the quick-thinking captain of the tug *Vulcan* who got stern ropes on her to stop her drift. At the same time, an equally quick-thinking Smith ordered "full astern" to stop *Titanic*'s forward motion, and the resulting backwash of water pushed *New York* away from *Titanic*'s stern.

By now, *New York*'s remaining mooring lines had broken and she started to drift downriver. Other tugs managed to get additional lines on *New York* and finally halted her drift past the end of the docks. With *New York* secured, Smith was given permission to proceed and, more than an hour late, *Titanic* recommenced her thirty-eight kilometre journey to the English Channel. En route, she passed the spot where *Olympic* and HMS *Hawke* had collided in an eerily similar situation to the one that had just occurred. Approaching the Channel, *Titanic* slowed to drop off the pilot and headed for the French port of Cherbourg, about a hundred kilometres away.

As the ship's bugler went from deck to deck summoning passengers to dinner, some people undoubtedly reflected on the near accident at Southampton. One of them—a stranger—voiced his opinion in strong terms to Irene Harris, the wife of New York theatre manager Henry Harris: "That was a bad omen. Get off this ship at Cherbourg, if we get that far. That's what I'm going to do." The maiden voyage of the world's largest ship had begun under less-than-auspicious circumstances.

A fully lit Titanic *departed Cherbourg two hours behind schedule.*

CHAPTER 3

PORTS OF CALL

CHERBOURG

TITANIC'S FIRST STOP WAS THE French port of Cherbourg, where 274 passengers who had taken the six-hour journey from Paris's Gare St. Lazare on the Train transatlantique were waiting to board the ship. Cherbourg, which had been the White Star Line's continental port since 1907 when it began its Southampton to New York service, was much smaller than Southampton and could not handle large liners. Consequently, passengers, their baggage, and several mailbags were taken to *Titanic* aboard two tenders. *Nomadic* and *Traffic* had been constructed at Harland and Wolff's Belfast yard in 1911 in order to be ready to assist the maiden voyage of *Olympic* that year.

Due to *Titanic's* near accident with *New York* while departing Southampton, the Cherbourg passengers reached their destination before she did and had to wait at the port's tiny Gare Maritime until the giant ship arrived at 6:30 P.M. *Nomadic* then ferried 142 first-class and 30 second-class passengers, while *Traffic* carried 102 third-class passengers and the mail to the waiting *Titanic*. Not realizing at the time how fortunate they were, 15 first-class and 9 second-class passengers, who had each paid between £1 and £3 for the voyage, disembarked at Cherbourg after their brief channel crossing. Among the first-class passengers who disembarked were Thomas and Clementina Dyer-Edwardes, the parents of Lucy, Countess of Rothes, on the way to their Normandy chateau. Their daughter was on her way to British Columbia to join her husband, who was investigating fruit farms there for investment.

Like those who got on at Southampton, the Cherbourg passengers were an eclectic lot, although perhaps somewhat more exotic because of several travellers from the Middle East. Among the first-class passengers was Lieutenant

John Jacob Astor was the wealthiest man aboard Titanic. *He was returning to New York with his much-younger second wife, Madeleine.*

Colonel John Jacob Astor IV, one of the wealthiest men in America and certainly the richest man aboard *Titanic*. He was heir to the vast fortune begun by his great-grandfather, John Jacob Astor, in opium, furs, and real estate. In 1909, John Jacob IV, then forty-five, had divorced his wife of eighteen years and mother to their two children.

At the time, divorce was considered a scandal (most men who could afford it simply took a mistress instead) and high society was shocked. When Astor announced that he would remarry, the scandal rebounded, especially when it was discovered that his new wife was eighteen-year-old Madeleine Talmadge Force, a woman a year younger than his son. The couple was largely snubbed by much of upper-class society. To avoid the gossip, Astor and his new bride took an extended honeymoon in Egypt and France. When Madeleine became pregnant during the trip, the Astors decided to return to the United States early so the baby could be born there. Accompanying the Astors were valet Victor Robbins, maid Rosalie Bidois, nurse Caroline Endres, and their beloved pet Airedale, Kitty. Astor was an accomplished individual. He had written a science fiction novel and patented several inventions, including a bicycle brake and a device to produce gas from peat moss. He was also a shrewd businessman who added millions to the Astor fortune through real estate.

One of the Americans who did not snub the Astors was Margaret Brown, later to be fictionalized in popular culture as "The Unsinkable Molly Brown." She had been travelling with the newlyweds on part of their trip and coincidentally was called home at the same time due to the illness of her first grandchild. At eighteen, Molly had moved from her Missouri home to Leadville, Colorado, where she met and married Jim Brown, usually known as J. J. Eventually, J. J.'s engineering efforts in developing an ore seam paid off and the Browns became wealthy. They moved to Denver, where Molly continued her earlier work in women's rights issues and where she developed an interest in the arts, among other areas. In 1909, Molly and J. J. separated and were never reconciled, although they remained friends. A cash settlement and a $700-a-month allowance permitted her to continue her social work and travel.

Philadelphians Charlotte Cardeza and her thirty-six-year-old son, Thomas, travelled in the second of *Titanic*'s two millionaire's three-room suites, each of which had its own private promenade. The Cardeza party included Charlotte's personal maid, Anna Ward, and Thomas's valet, Gustave Lesueur. The Cardeza's luggage consisted of fourteen trunks, four suitcases, and three baggage crates, which were to figure prominently in the disaster's aftermath. Another wealthy Philadelphian was forty-six-year-old mining and smelting magnate Benjamin Guggenheim, nicknamed the "Silver Prince." One of the most prominent Americans aboard *Titanic*, Guggenheim was accompanied by his valet, Victor Giglio, and his chauffeur, René Pernot, who travelled in second class. An additional member of the party was twenty-four-year-old Parisian singer, Ninette Aubart, who was accompanied by her Swiss maid, Emma Sägesser. Ninette was Guggenheim's mistress and occupied a cabin not far from her lover's.

Guggenheim did not possess his father's business sense, and frittered away much of his inherited fortune in bad investments. Although he married in 1894 and had three daughters, he subsequently grew distant from his wife and was frequently away from their New York home, often staying at his Paris apartment. Guggenheim had originally booked passage on the Cunarder *Lusitania*, but when her sailing was cancelled for repairs, rather than take *Carmania*, the Cunard Line's replacement for *Lusitania*, he switched to *Titanic* for her maiden voyage.

One of the more controversial couples who emerged in the subsequent inquiries that followed the *Titanic* disaster was Sir Cosmo Duff-Gordon and his wife, Lady Duff-Gordon. Sir Cosmo was the fifth baronet (the only hereditary honour that is not a peerage; baronets are commoners and not noblemen) of the Halkin baronetcy that had been created in 1813. He was a prominent Scottish landowner and sportsman, particularly fencing. His wife, Lucy, a divorcee and the daughter of a Toronto engineer, was a famous London fashion designer known as "Madame Lucile." Because of her lack of financial skills, Lucy had taken Sir Cosmo on as a business partner, a relationship that resulted in their marriage.

For some unknown reason, the Duff-Gordons signed onto *Titanic* as Mr. and Mrs. Morgan and had separate cabins. Lady Lucy's secretary, Laura Fracatelli, travelled with the Duff-Gordons and stayed in another cabin. In her autobiography, Lucy claimed that they had not originally intended to sail on *Titanic*, but

LEFT *Mining magnate Benjamin Guggenheim was travelling aboard* Titanic *with his mistress.* RIGHT *Lady Lucy and her husband, Sir Cosmo Duff-Gordon, registered under assumed names and had separate cabins aboard* Titanic.

that urgent business in New York required her to take the first available ship. Because of her work, the Duff-Gordons often lived apart and Lucy maintained a Paris apartment and a Versailles summer villa.

Helen Churchill Candee was an American from a family of means who had divorced her wealthy yet abusive husband. Despite offers of financial help from well-off family members and friends, Helen shocked them and decided to support herself as a writer. She succeeded, and became a popular author and lecturer on many subjects, including the liberal arts, home decor, and East Asia.

The only black person aboard *Titanic* was Haitian Joseph Laroche, who had settled in Paris, received an engineering degree, and married a Frenchwoman, Juliette Lafargue. After his wife gave birth to two daughters, Laroche decided to return to Haiti because racial discrimination had kept him from high-paying jobs. Among the other passengers were two Spanish-speaking businessmen. Uruguayan Ramon Artagaveytia was on his way home to Montevideo, while Spaniard Servando Ovies y Rodriguez was en route to his company in Havana, Cuba.

CANADIANS

THE BAXTER FAMILY of Montreal was staying in the suite beside Ismay's on B Deck. The group consisted of Hélène, the widow of disgraced diamond broker and banker James "Diamond Jim" Baxter, and two of her three children: twenty-seven-year-old married daughter Mary Douglas and twenty-four-year-old son Quigg. Diamond Jim had already made a lot of money in general brokerage services when, in 1892, he opened the Baxter Block on St. Lawrence Boulevard, a far-sighted development that put twenty-eight stores under one roof—perhaps Canada's first true shopping mall (notwithstanding the claims of several other "first" shopping malls across the country). In 1900 he was accused of violating U.S. currency exchange regulations and found guilty later that year of defrauding his own bank. He died shortly after being released from prison in 1905.

Although the family's circumstances were diminished, it was by no means poor. Jim had left Hélène several investments in France, Belgium, and Switzerland, which required her to make annual trips in the fall to Europe to check on them. She typically remained overseas until the spring. On this occasion she took Mary (nicknamed "Zette"—short for one of her three middle names, Suzette) and Quigg with her. Zette was married to Dr. Fred Douglas, who had treated her brother's eye injury caused by a blow from a stick in a hockey game. (As a result of the injury, Quigg lost the sight in his left eye.) Despite their wealth, the half-French, half-Irish, Catholic, French-speaking Baxters were not accepted by Montreal's Scottish Presbyterian elite and were social outsiders.

There was another member of the Baxter party, but she was known only to Quigg. Travelling under the name of Mrs. B. De Villiers, Berthe Mayné was a Belgian cabaret singer and courtesan well-known in Brussels among those who "like to wine and dine and enjoy life." She and Quigg had met in the Belgian capital in the winter of 1911 and quickly began a passionate love affair. Whether she was travelling with Quigg to continue the affair or had already received a proposal of marriage from him will never be known. In any case, for the sake of propriety, Quigg had installed her in her own first-class cabin on c Deck, conveniently located near the first-class entrance stairwell.

Albert Mallet, his wife, Antoinine, and their two-year-old son, André, had boarded at Cherbourg. The French family had been visiting relatives in Paris and were returning to Montreal, where Albert worked for a Canadian liquor company as a cognac importer. Travelling with the Mallets was family friend Emile Richard, who had just finished his compulsory service with the French army. Emile's father was sending him on a six-month vacation in Canada before he started to work at the family distillery.

Several new or prospective Canadians from the Middle East who boarded at Cherbourg were travelling third class. Many came from the village of Kfar Mishki in Lebanon, which was not yet an independent country but part of Syria at the time. At least a dozen were headed for Ottawa. Mariana Assaf already lived there and was returning after visiting two sons she had left behind. Travelling with her were two younger relatives, cousin Gerios Assaf and nephew Solomon Khalil. Khalil had gone home in search of a wife, but was returning without one. Joseph Caram, an Ottawa merchant, was successful in a similar quest and was travelling with his teenage bride, Maria. Accompanying the newlyweds were Maria's father, Joseph Elias, and two brothers, Joseph Jr. (fifteen) and Tannous (twenty-two). Others in the Kfar Mishki group were Catherine Barbara and her travelling companion (possibly a daughter), Saiide, as well as Ottawa journalists Mansour Hanna and Mansour Novel (also spelled Nofal), both of whom had left their families behind in Syria. Sultani Boulos and her two children, Nourelain (seven) and Akar (nine), were joining her husband in Ontario. Travelling alone were Elias (twelve) and Jamila (fourteen) Nicola-Yarred. Their father had not been allowed to proceed because of an eye infection, so he sent the two ahead with some relatives. All but Mariana Assaf and the Nicola-Yarred children perished in the sinking.

Six Armenians were travelling together from the village of Keghi in Turkish Armenia. Ortin Zakarian, Maprie Der Zakarian, Neshan Krekorian, Sarkis Mardirosian, Orsen Sirayanian, and David Vartanian, all Christians, were fleeing Turkish Muslim persecution and looking forward to a new life in Brantford, Ontario. Neshan complained of being "cooped up like a chicken" in his third-class cabin.

QUEENSTOWN

AT 8:00 P.M., ninety minutes after her arrival, *Titanic* winched in her anchor and left Cherbourg, headed for her last stop, Queenstown, Ireland (today known as Cobh—the Cove (of Cork) in English). As she left the French port she was fully illuminated. The ship arrived off Queenstown early on the morning of April 12 and dropped anchor off Roches Point, about three kilometres from the dock, at 11:30. As at Cherbourg, two small tenders, *America* and *Ireland* in this case, ferried passengers, luggage, and mail to and from shore.

Altogether, 123 passengers boarded at Queenstown: 3 first-class, 7 second-class, and 93 third-class. Only 44 of them would survive the sinking. As the two tenders carried passengers and 1,385 mailbags out to the waiting ship, a number of smaller vessels accompanied them carrying local vendors selling various items, such as lace and other crafts, to wealthy passengers. Astor, for example, bought some lace for his wife. Officially, seven people—all first-class passengers—disembarked, but there was an eighth person who also got off. Fireman/stoker John Coffey, who had been born in Queenstown, hid under the mailbags being taken ashore and so escaped the disaster.

Among the seven passengers who disembarked legally was amateur photographer Francis Browne, a theological student studying to be a Jesuit priest. Browne's

Dr. William Minahan and his family were the only first-class passengers to board at Queenstown.

hobby resulted in an invaluable photographic record of *Titanic's* maiden voyage from Southampton to Queenstown, including pictures of the near mishap with *New York*, several passengers, and the last known photograph of Captain Smith. Browne's uncle, the Bishop of Cloyne, who resided in Queenstown, had given him both the camera and the *Titanic* ticket.

The three first-class passengers who boarded were the Minahans from Wisconsin. Dr. William Minahan was the son of Irish immigrants and had been visiting his parent's homeland, along with his wife, Lillian, and his younger sister, Daisy. Among Queenstown's second-class passengers were two with Canadian destinations. Hilda Slayter of Halifax was returning to Canada after purchasing her wedding trousseau in England, while the Reverend Charles Kirkland, a Presbyterian minister from Glasgow, was travelling to Saskatchewan to visit his sister. He would not live to see her.

Slayter was the daughter of a Halifax doctor. When her lack of sufficient talent ended her dreams of a singing career, she accepted a proposal of marriage from the son of an English baron living in British Columbia and went to England to purchase her trousseau, a fairly common undertaking by females of a certain class at the time. Among her baggage were trunks containing "one satin opal and pearl wedding dress with silver opal and mesh scarf, satin slippers, silk stockings and a hair bandeau," as well as a "blue satin silver dress, silver and blue scarf, silver tissue and osprey and Italian embroidered lace hand made blouses."

The vast majority of passengers who embarked at Queenstown were travelling in steerage. Although some had been born in Ireland, immigrated to the United States earlier, and had returned to Ireland to visit family and friends, most were first-time emigrants. A group led by Katherine McGowan combined both of these. She had immigrated to America earlier and was travelling back to Chicago with her niece, leading nearly a dozen County Mayo emigrants. Many other emigrants also travelled together, such as a party of six led by Daniel Buckley, or in smaller groups of two or three friends or relatives. McGowan died while Buckley survived.

About a dozen of the third-class passengers were headed for Canada, many of them joining relatives who already lived there. Orangeman Thomas Morrow was leaving County Down to join his brother as a hand on a ranch near Gleichen, Alberta, where he hoped to make his fortune. Brigit O'Sullivan, from County Cork, was convinced by her brother who lived in Montreal that the city offered young women better opportunities than Ireland did. Railway station porter Patrick Colbert from County Limerick was also going to Quebec to join his brother as a monk in a monastery in Sherbrooke. All three perished and their bodies were not recovered. An obituary in the *Cork Examiner* of April 22 stated that Colbert was "noted for his industry, intelligence and temperate habits." As so many of their countrymen had done previously, these men and women were hoping to leave the hardscrabble existence of life in Ireland and make new lives in the New World.

TOTAL PASSENGERS

EVEN TODAY, THERE is some dispute about how many people actually were aboard *Titanic* when she left Queenstown. Part of this is due to the record-keeping at the time; no computers cranked out last-minute changes to passenger and crew lists. On the passenger side, some people booked and then didn't show up, yet were still counted as being aboard. Others showed up at the last minute without a ticket and bought one just before sailing, never to be listed. Several others sailed under false names, so their true identity has never been known. The names of many third-class emigrants were mangled by White Star Line staff or immigration personnel, with various spellings for the same person, as well as first and last names reversed.

The generally accepted estimate for the total number of people aboard *Titanic* is 2,229. Passengers included 325 first-class, 285 second-class, and 706 third-class for a total of 1,316. The cost of tickets varied greatly. In general terms, a first class parlour suite cost £870, while a first class berth was £30. Second class accommodation was £12 and third class was £3 to £8. Sharing a cabin with someone else saved 40 percent of the fare.

CREW

EVEN HARDER THAN ascertaining passenger numbers is establishing the number of crew aboard *Titanic*. As for passengers, there are several reasons for this. Some crew had signed on for the voyage, but never showed up. Last-minute replacements were hired at Southampton, but some of their names were never recorded. Perhaps a better name than crew is non-passengers, because of several people that operated in a nether world between passengers and crew and were not considered as either. Best estimates put the number of non-passengers aboard the vessel as 913. Wages for crew varied considerably. At the top, Captain Smith earned £1,250 per year (plus a no-collision bonus of £200), while the lowliest crew members, such as scullions and stewardesses, made monthly wages of

£3 and 10 shillings—paid only for the period actually signed on a ship's crew. In 1912, Southampton had a population of 120,000. The majority of crew members came from the city, while most of those not employed directly by the shipping lines had their livelihood influenced by the industry. Due to the coal strike, few ships had sailed in early 1912, so White Star officials could choose the best of seventeen thousand unemployed men and women for *Titanic*.

No matter what their status in society, their personal wealth, or their position in the functioning of the ship, the fate of all 2,229 souls aboard *Titanic* largely rested on the skill, experience, and capabilities of the 60 or so men who made up the ship's officers and deck crew, some of whom were found wanting. Yet, for the next three and a half days, life on board *Titanic* for most passengers was idyllic. How quickly that would change.

AT SEA

AT 1:30 P.M. ON April 11, 1912, the tenders and *Titanic* exchanged whistles, indicating that the smaller ships were ready to return to port. The big ship weighed anchor as third-class passenger and farm labourer Eugene Daly played "Erin's Lament" and "A Nation Once Again" for his fellow steerage passengers on his uileann, or traditional Irish elbow pipes. *Titanic* came about and set a course into the broad Atlantic, leaving her last port of call receding in the distance. The ship was now four hours behind schedule. As officers and crew settled into the routines that governed every minute of the voyage, passengers familiarized

Passengers enjoy a walk around the boat, or promenade, deck, where Titanic's *lifeboats hung in their davits.*

Titanic *sails on her maiden voyage.*

⁂

WRECK OF THE TITAN

In 1898, American author Morgan Robertson wrote a short novel originally titled *Futility*, which eerily foreshadowed events surrounding the *Titanic* tragedy. Robertson's book is about the largest ship afloat at the time, *Titan*, which is considered unsinkable. *Titan* crashes into an iceberg in the North Atlantic about 650 kilometres from Newfoundland on her maiden voyage in April and sinks with considerable loss of life, partly due to insufficient lifeboats. The similarities between the two ships, one imaginary and one real, and their fate—some fourteen years apart—is remarkable.

Morgan wrote his novella nine years before the Olympic class was even conceived. Among the similarities between *Titan* and *Titanic* were registry: British; displacement: 45,000 tons/66,000 tons (respectively); horsepower: 40,000/46,000; length: 268 metres/269 metres; propellers: 3; top speed: 25 knots/24 knots; watertight bulkheads: 19/15; lifeboats: 24/20; passengers: 3,000/2,229; time of impact: near midnight/11:40 P.M.; and point of impact: starboard. Robertson rewrote his book after the *Titanic* disaster, leading to accusations that he was trying to make money from it. Although he made some notable changes, including the new title of *Wreck of the Titan*, the similarities above remained unchanged. Robertson died in 1915.

themselves with the ship. In an age when shipboard activities (except for meals and church services) were not arranged for passengers, they quickly formed their own routines of walking, talking, playing games, reading, and sleeping. As it turned out, there was not very much time to enjoy shipboard life aboard the massive new vessel.

During the first three days of her intended transatlantic crossing (traditionally measured from noon to noon), *Titanic* registered 621 kilometres on Friday, 835 kilometres on Saturday, and 878.5 kilometres on Sunday. If these distances had remained constant, *Titanic* would have arrived in New York early on Wednesday morning. As was the custom, many male passengers made bets on the distance to be covered on Monday and Tuesday, as well as the exact arrival time in New York. An enduring myth about *Titanic* is that she was going faster than conditions warranted in an attempt to establish a transatlantic speed record. Some versions have Captain Smith responsible for this, while others state it was ordered by Ismay.

While it is true that the ship was travelling faster than she should have after ice was reported, this was the accepted practice at the time for some ships' captains. They thought the best way to cross areas where ice was present was to steam full ahead in an attempt to get out of the danger area as soon as possible. Surprisingly, the theory worked in practice most times—but not for *Titanic*. In any case, given her size it would have been impossible for *Titanic* to set a new transatlantic record. Her service speed was 21 knots, far below the top speed of the fast Cunarders that held the Blue Riband for record crossing times.

An iceberg drifts in the North Atlantic.

CHAPTER 4

DISASTER

ICE

OF ALL THE DANGERS TO SHIPPING in the North Atlantic at the time, perhaps the greatest was ice, either in the form of three-to-six-metre-thick sheet ice or icebergs of any size, from growlers (less than a metre visible above water and less than five metres wide) to very large (more than seventy-five metres visible above water and more than two hundred metres wide). Due to an uncommonly mild winter in 1911–1912, more icebergs than normal had broken off from the Greenland ice shelf and drifted south into North Atlantic shipping lanes. On encountering ice, ships should have adopted low speeds, manoeuvred constantly, and travelled primarily in daylight. Even before she departed Southampton, *Titanic*'s radio operators received warnings about ice in her track from at least twenty other ships. On Sunday, the first warning arrived at 9:00 A.M. and was followed by a steady stream of additional ones. Unbelievably, some of these did not get passed to the bridge officers.

At 10:00 P.M. lookouts Frederick Fleet and Reginald Lee began their watch high up in the open crow's nest on the foremast. The temperature had dropped considerably during the evening to about -1°C and the lookouts had been told to watch for icebergs. By this time, *Titanic* was already inside an extensive icefield, unseen because of the dark, moonless night. While the lookouts tried to keep warm in the biting cold, their visibility problem was compounded by the lack of binoculars in the crow's nest—unknowingly secured in a locker in Lightoller's cabin.

The last ice warning to *Titanic* came from the steamship *Californian*, stopped in the middle of an icefield a few kilometres away for the night, on orders of Captain Stanley Lord. Wireless operator Cyril Evans, using the informal "old man" appellation for unofficial traffic, signalled "We are stopped and surrounded by ice." Even before the message was completed, Jack Phillips aboard *Titanic* cut into the transmission with "Keep out! Shut up! You're jamming my signal. I'm working Cape Race." Snubbed, Evans did not try to contact *Titanic* again, shut down his wireless, and went to bed. The argument continues to the present day over whether Captain Lord later ignored *Titanic* when some of his officers and crew told him of seeing eight white rockets rising into the night sky.

THE FIRST EIGHTY MINUTES

AT 11:40 P.M. THE CROW'S nest lookouts had only twenty minutes left in their watch when Fleet spotted something looming out of the water dead ahead. He immediately rang the crow's nest bell three times as he called the bridge on the ship's phone. "Iceberg right ahead!" he shouted to Sixth Officer Moody. On the bridge, Moody repeated the warning to First Officer Murdoch, who ordered the engines stopped and then reversed on the engine room telegraph as he yelled at quartermaster Robert Hichens "Hard-a-starboard!" in an attempt to avoid a collision. It didn't work. *Titanic*'s forward starboard hull scraped along a few hundred metres of rock-hard underwater ice, causing a series of holes, bent plates, and popped rivets, which allowed the first five watertight compartments to begin flooding. As Hichens spun the wheel, Murdoch threw the switches that closed fifteen watertight doors on the lowest deck, known as the tank top.

Marconi
Wires

Submerged shelf
of iceberg

Chart
House

Bridge

1ˢᵗ Point of Contact
with Ice

4
Forward
Boats

Submerged shelf of Iceberg

Boat Deck

4 Stern
Boats

Starboard side

Direction of Iceberg
after contact

Submerged Bulk of Iceberg

A contemporary artist's depiction of Titanic *hitting the iceberg.*

To passengers and crew that felt or heard the collision, it did not seem like much. Mrs. Ella White described the sensation "as though we went over about a thousand marbles," while Victor Sunderland heard a sound "similar to that a basket of coal would make if dropped on an iron plate." Many people did not even wake up or, if they did, promptly went back to sleep. Haligonian George Wright, for example, was known to be a deep sleeper and speculation is that he may have remained soundly asleep in his cabin until it was too late to get out. Captain

Marconi wireless operator Jack Phillips sent Titanic's *distress calls, including the last. Although he made it to a lifeboat, Phillips did not survive.*

Smith arrived on the bridge moments later and ordered various inspections to determine the degree of damage, if any. The initial results were not good.

Smith ordered the now-stopped ship "half ahead," an action that allowed tons of additional seawater to pour into the ship as he made his own inspection. Ten minutes later, after he had returned to the bridge, he ordered *Titanic* stopped for the last time. To prevent the boilers from exploding, the ship's engine room crew vented steam through the escape valves in each funnel. The noise was ear shattering and prevented any conversation on deck. It also woke most of the passengers and crew still asleep. *Titanic* was built to stay afloat with four forward compartments flooded; with five flooding she was doomed. The watertight compartments only went as high as D or E Deck, so when water reached the top of one, it spilled over into the next compartment—the so-called "ice cube tray effect." When designer Thomas Andrews estimated the stricken ship had "An hour and a half. Possibly two. Not much longer," in response to Smith's question, the captain passed the ship's position to Phillips and told him to send out a distress signal. Twenty-five minutes had elapsed since the ship struck the iceberg.

CARPATHIA

THE ROYAL MAIL SHIP *Carpathia* was a Cunard Line vessel built in Newcastle-upon-Tyne in northeast England and launched in August 1902 for the transatlantic passenger trade, initially sailing on the Liverpool-Queenstown-Boston run. She was 170 metres long and displaced 8,600 tons. After successful sea trials, *Carpathia* commenced her maiden voyage on May 5, 1903, and was eventually transferred to the New York-Trieste-Fiume route, where she carried immigrants—mainly Hungarian—to America. *Carpathia* could carry 2,550 passengers.

Carpathia, *the only ship to rescue* Titanic's *survivors.*

Around midnight on Sunday, Harold Cottam, the lone wireless operator aboard *Carpathia*, was tired and ready for bed. Ever since the ship left New York on April 11—bound for the Mediterranean ports of Gibraltar, Genoa, Naples, Trieste, and Fiume with 725 passengers and cargo—Cottam had been trying to keep up with a large volume of incoming and outgoing message traffic. After seventeen straight hours with only a short lunch break he was still up, waiting for a message from the liner *Parisian* confirming receipt of one he had sent earlier. In preparation for his well-deserved sleep, Cottam had removed his shoes and some of this clothing.

Tired, a little bored, and still waiting for *Parisian*'s reply, the youthful wireless operator switched frequencies to other stations to see if anything of interest was being sent. He picked up Cape Cod, which was transmitting commercial messages to *Titanic* that went unanswered. Cottam copied down several of the messages, hoping to send them to *Titanic* in the morning. With still no reply from *Parisian*, Cottam switched to *Titanic*'s frequency, but heard nothing. On speculation, he sent a message to *Titanic*. It was a transmission that had far-reaching results and led to the dramatic rescue of hundreds of people:

> Carpathia: *"I say, old man, do you know there is a batch of messages coming through for you from MCC [Cape Cod]?"*
> Titanic *(breaking into* Carpathia's *transmission)*: *"Come at once. We have struck a berg, It's a CQD [international distress signal], O[ld] M[an]. Position 41° 46' N, 50° 14' W."*
> Carpathia: *"Shall I tell my captain? Do you require assistance?*
> Titanic: *"Yes. Come quick."*

Grabbing his jacket, Cottam raced to the bridge and passed the message to the officer on duty, First Officer H. V. Dean. Without hesitation, Dean pushed Cottam out of the bridge and down the stairs to the captain's cabin, where he burst through the door without knocking. Captain Arthur Rostron, who had just gone to bed, was a stickler for discipline and not amused by the disruption. He demanded to know the reason. After Dean had Cottam repeat the message, Rostron asked, "Are you certain?" When the wireless operator replied affirmatively, Rostron immediately went to the chart room, where he calculated the course, distance, and time to *Titanic*. If Rostron pushed his elderly vessel beyond her maximum rated speed of 14 knots, say to an unheard-of 17 knots, he figured could cover the ninety-three kilometres to *Titanic* in about four and a half hours. *Carpathia*'s captain unhesitatingly ordered his ship to turn northwest and

Much of Titanic*'s tragedy played out on her boat deck.*

proceed at full speed. But could he get to the stricken *Titanic*'s side before the giant ship went under?

Captain Smith's actions—or more specifically, lack of them—indicate that he was overwhelmed by the enormity of what was happening to his ship, perhaps not even believing that such a calamity could transpire. Speaking in 1907 about the maiden voyage of *Adriatic*, he said, "I cannot imagine any condition which would cause a ship to founder. I cannot conceive of any vital disaster happening to this vessel. Modern shipbuilding has gone beyond that." Yet, here was his very own ship, the largest in the world, said by some to be unsinkable, going down by the head. Most eyewitness accounts of the captain's behaviour clearly suggest that Smith was virtually paralyzed into inactivity and gave little guidance, direction, or orders to his officers after his initial direction regarding the lifeboats. At first, only a handful of people likely knew the true extent of *Titanic*'s dangerous situation. It was probably not until midnight, some twenty minutes after hitting the iceberg that the captain gave the order to Chief Officer Wilde to uncover the lifeboats. Wilde promptly delegated the responsibility to Second Officer Lightoller.

REARRANGING THE DECK CHAIRS ON *TITANIC*

The aphorism "rearranging the deck chairs on the *Titanic*" is fairly well established in popular culture, but surprisingly it is not as old as some people think. The phrase refers to doing something insignificant or pointless that will soon be overtaken by events, or that contributes nothing to the solution of a problem. Initially, the editors of the *Oxford Dictionary of Quotations* ascribed it to U.S. President Gerald Ford's campaign manager, who was quoted in the *Washington Post* on May 16, 1976, saying, "I'm not going to rearrange the furniture on the deck of the *Titanic*," in reference to losing five of six primary elections. Later, the editors found an earlier use of the phrase in the *New York Times* of May 15, 1972, which stated, "Administrators [at the Lincoln Center] are running around straightening out deck chairs while the *Titanic* goes down."

Lightoller proceeded to Lifeboat 4, directing crewmen by hand signals because of the noise of escaping steam from the funnels. As additional sailors showed up, he moved along the deck to the other lifeboats, while First Officer Murdoch started with the boats on the other side. Five or so minutes later Smith ordered the lifeboats swung out. The direction to begin loading the lifeboats most likely came shortly after 12:25 A.M. In the absence of any public address system or warning bells, stewards were sent throughout the ship to knock on each cabin and ensure its occupants were awake.

First-class passengers were told to put on warm clothing and a lifebelt and go to the boat deck, while second-class passengers were directed to the dining saloon. For third-class passengers, it was more problematic. Stewards opened the cabin doors with their pass keys, grabbed the lifebelts off the top shelf, dumped them on the floor, and shouted for everyone to put them on. Some authors have tried to make the point that the many non-English speakers aboard were essentially left on their own to figure out what was happening. But this is a bit disingenuous. Conversation was nearly impossible in any case, and the sight of lifebelts being thrown on the floor and English speakers all around them putting them on would surely have spoken louder than any words. Only the most obtuse individuals could not have figured out what was happening.

ALTHOUGH THE WHITE STAR Line's orders to its captains directed that a lifeboat drill be held every Sunday morning, for some reason Smith never conducted one at any time during the voyage. Additionally, no instructions were posted stating who should report to what lifeboat, or how to wear a lifebelt. In fairness to Smith, such oversights were fairly common at the time. While the captain did not find the time to perform the duty of a lifeboat drill, he did somehow find the time to see to the spiritual needs of his passengers and personally conducted a religious service on Sunday morning, at 10:30 in the first-class dining saloon. It was the only opportunity that third-class passengers had to see a first-class area.

Titanic carried twenty lifeboats of three different types: fourteen standard lifeboats with a capacity of sixty-five persons each, two emergency lifeboats that could carry forty people each, and four Englehardt collapsible lifeboats with folding canvas sides that could each hold forty-seven. The total capacity of all types was 1,178, or 53 percent of those aboard. Despite this shortfall, the ship was fully compliant with British Board of Trade regulations at the time, which stated that the largest vessels needed enough lifeboats to carry about 960 persons. Unbelievably, *Titanic* actually exceeded the Board of Trade's regulations. They had been designed for a time when it was never imagined that ships might reach *Titanic*'s sixty-six thousand tons and had not been updated since 1894, when the largest ships reached ten thousand tons.

Ironically, the giant vessel had the potential capacity to carry sixty-four lifeboats using new, larger Welin davits capable of holding up to four boats each, which would have held everybody aboard on her maiden voyage.

The new type of davits installed on Titanic *could have carried up to sixty-four lifeboats, enough to get all passengers and crew away safely.*

Families say goodbye to their men while Titanic's crew try to organize the lifeboats.

Unfortunately, White Star management (many sources suggest J. Bruce Ismay himself) rejected the larger number, believing that additional lifeboats would spoil the ship's graceful lines. Tragically, if all of *Titanic*'s existing lifeboats had been filled to capacity, an additional 465 lives would have been saved. Full lifeboats could have easily carried all 537 women and children aboard, as well as 641 men. As it turned out, 162 women and children perished and 375 were saved, while 1,354 men died and only 338 were rescued.

Sadly, many men and boys five or older were needlessly denied the opportunity to enter partially filled lifeboats by personal interpretation of the term "women and children *first.*" On the starboard side, First Officer Murdoch was in charge of loading the boats. He followed the rule explicitly and only allowed male passengers to enter a lifeboat if there were no other women or children in the immediate area. If there was still room, he then allowed male crew members to get in. On the port side, where Second Officer Lightoller was in charge, his interpretation was different and he believed that he was to load women and children *only*. This more rigid understanding of the rule resulted in several lifeboats leaving with empty seats, even if men were nearby. Paradoxically, Lightoller survived.

THE FIRST LIFEBOATS

There remain many unknowns around the sinking of *Titanic*. Since the disaster, several questions have been answered, but many more remain unresolved. It is highly doubtful that the answers to all of them will be discovered. Although the presumed sequence and departure times of *Titanic*'s twenty lifeboats were published in a table in the final report of the British inquiry into the disaster, the American inquiry remained silent on this matter. Comparing the British inquiry's table with the transcribed testimony of survivors and separate personal accounts reveals several inconsistencies and errors. Over the years, various researchers have reached different conclusions regarding the actual timings of the lifeboat launchings. One researcher, Senan Molony, argues that the first lifeboat was lowered away twenty minutes earlier than previously thought. The lifeboat timings that follow are based largely on the meticulous research of Bill Wormstedt, Tad Fitch, and George Behe and represent some of latest conclusions.

By 12:30, a few passengers had arrived on the boat deck and stood around the lifeboats. The cold and the noise of escaping steam soon drove them indoors either to the first-class entrance or the gymnasium. At the same time, some of the wealthiest passengers aboard had gathered one deck below on A Deck, where

Ismay's design change kept them warm behind the glass panels he had ordered installed to keep ocean spray out. With their comfort in mind, stewards had told the group to wait there until the lifeboats were lowered to A Deck, where they would then be able to get in them. Among the group were several millionaires, including the Astors, Wideners, and Thayers, along with their servants. Second Officer Lightoller had Lifeboat 4 swung out and lowered to A Deck, only to discover that the new windows could only be opened with a special tool that could not be found. Lightoller told the group to wait until the tool was found, when he would return. Without a word, some of the richest people in the world followed his direction and calmly waited on the sinking ship for someone to return with the tool.

When John Jacob Astor told his wife, Madeleine, that *Titanic* had hit an iceberg but that it was not serious, she took the time to dress properly—for going out in public. She put on a silk purple suit with a button-down skirt, a mink collar, and a fur wrap. For jewellery, she put on a ruby and emerald necklace, followed by a diamond necklace, a string of pearls, pearl earrings, a diamond watch, four pearl bracelets, plus her wedding ring, engagement ring, and a few other rings. On the way out of their suite, she grabbed a mink purse, stuffed it with $200 and a few more jewels, and proceeded to the boat deck.

12:40

ONE HOUR AFTER hitting the iceberg, starboard Lifeboat 7 was the first lifeboat lowered into the water. It was under Murdoch's control and had lookout George Hogg in charge. At this stage, most people did not believe *Titanic* would sink, so only a total of twenty-eight people got in it: twelve male and twelve female first-class passengers, a male second-class passenger, and three crewmen. As it later turned out, most of the deck crew survived because they manned the lifeboats, and working on the upper decks also gave them easier access to the lifeboats. Lifeboat 7, ordered to remain around the forward gangway door, only did so for a few minutes before the crewmen rowed it about two hundred metres off the starboard side. As *Titanic* began her final plunge, they rowed farther away to avoid the anticipated suction.

Among the occupants of Lifeboat 7 was sculptor Paul Chevré, who later stated he had been ordered into the lifeboat "to set an example" for other passengers. Chevré was interviewed by a *Montreal Herald* reporter on arrival in New York, who produced a fantastic story. In it, Chevré stated that his bust of Sir Wilfrid

THE BIRKENHEAD DRILL

The tradition of allowing women and children to leave a sinking ship before the men began with the troopship HMS *Birkenhead*. In 1852, she was carrying 634 people off the South African coast, most of them soldiers of the 73rd Regiment, as well as a number of officers' families. In the early morning hours of February 25, at the appropriately-named Danger Point, the ship ran into a sunken reef, which tore a huge gash in her hull. Water poured in, drowning several soldiers instantly.

When surviving soldiers, sailors, and families gathered on the deck, the ship's captain and the 73rd's commanding officer calmly took charge. As only three of eight lifeboats were seaworthy, men silently stood back to allow women and children to board the lifeboats. The men remained on the deck as the ship broke up and sank, a mere twenty-five minutes after smashing into the rock.

That morning, a schooner arrived and rescued those in the lifeboats, men clinging to *Birkenhead*'s topmast, and the few who made it to shore. Only 193 survived the wreck, including every woman and child, while 445 men perished. Rudyard Kipling immortalized the heroism of the men aboard *Birkenhead* in his poem, "Sailor an' Soldier Too," exemplified in the lines "But stand an' be still to the Birken'ead drill is a damn tough bullet to chew." For many, the Birkenhead Drill symbolized the British characteristics of stoicism, fortitude, coolness under fire, and death before dishonour. As their actions proved, not all men aboard *Titanic* subscribed to its principles.

Laurier destined for the lobby of Ottawa's Chateau Laurier went down with the ship. He was also quoted as saying "a few minutes before the ship sank Captain Smith cried out, 'My luck has turned,' and then shot himself. I saw him fall against the canvas railing on the bridge and disappear." Chevré was upset at this gross fabrication and vehemently denied he had ever made such far-fetched comments. Among the other occupants of Lifeboat 7 was American actress Dorothy Gibson, who was travelling with her mother. Dorothy co-wrote and starred in a movie about *Titanic*, which was released a month after the tragedy. In it, she purportedly wore the same dress she had on when the ship sank.

A full lifeboat hangs in its davits prior to being lowered. This fanciful drawing shows the lifeboat in front of and below the bridge, when in fact all lifeboats were behind the bridge and on the same deck.

LIFEBOAT 5, THE SECOND lifeboat to be lowered, was also from the starboard side. Best estimates put the total number aboard it at least thirty-six, although it could have been as high as forty-one. There were thirteen male, fourteen female, and one child among the first-class passengers, plus six male and two female crew members. Third Officer Pitman was in charge, having been ordered into the boat by Murdoch so he could assist with any swimmers who might end up in the water either by jumping or falling in accidentally. For some reason, Ismay decided to help load this lifeboat. He even convinced a stewardess to "Jump in," although she did not think she was entitled to a place in the boat. As the boat was being lowered, Ismay shouted, "Lower away! Lower away!" much to the annoyance of Fifth Officer Harold Lowe, who yelled at him to "get the hell out of the way!" Ismay meekly complied and quickly walked away. Instead of picking up swimmers, however, the crew in Lifeboat 5 rowed about two hundred metres away and waited. When Pitman tried to return, he was shouted down by several women in the boat, who questioned why they should risk losing their lives "in a useless attempt to save others from the ship."

At about the same time, Fourth Officer Boxhall had the first of eight rockets fired, which climbed to 250 metres before bursting into a pattern of twelve white stars with a loud bang. Shortly before he had it fired, Boxhall thought he saw the lights of another ship in the distance, close enough to make out her masthead lights with binoculars. He hoped the rocket would attract her attention. Eventually, Boxhall and other crew members could see her red and green marker lights with the naked eye, which meant it was less than eight kilometres away. Inexplicably, the other ship turned around and sailed away. The identity of this mystery ship continues to be the subject of intense scrutiny to this day.

12:50

BELOW DECKS, pressure from seawater in bulkhead 6 collapsed a wall, instantly filling the adjacent boiler room No. 5 with water and drowning everyone inside except for one fireman, who escaped up a ladder. The collapse of this bulkhead was critical and accelerated *Titanic*'s demise. It may have been weakened by the coal fire that had smouldered for days before being extinguished. Meanwhile, a few decks above in the third-class areas, one of the finest acts of heroism that night was taking place. Steward John Hart and a couple of other crewmen bravely

A lifeboat rows away from the rapidly-sinking Titanic *as a passenger in the water cries out to be picked up.*

led about thirty third-class women and children through a maze of second- and first-class passageways to the boat deck.

12:55

BETWEEN THIRTY-EIGHT and forty people were in Lifeboat 3 when it was lowered from the starboard side. Passengers included one child, eight female, and ten male first-class passengers, along with one male and five first-class female servants, and a surprisingly high number of crewmen—thirteen. Among them were the Cardeza group: Charlotte, and her son, Thomas, as well as Charlotte's maid and Thomas's servant. Charles Hays, Thornton Davidson, and Vivian Payne assisted Hays's wife, Clara, and daughter, Orian (Thornton's wife) into the lifeboat, along with Clara's maid, Anne Perreault. Once all the available women were loaded, Murdoch offered available seats to the men and several got in, mostly crewmen. Davidson, Hays, Payne, and some other men remained on deck and went to help elsewhere. All perished. One of the male passengers who did get in was Bert Dick, escorted personally to the lifeboat, along with his wife, by Thomas Andrews. Once he was safely back home in Calgary, Dick was ostracized for surviving and even faced accusations that he had dressed as a woman to escape.

1:00

LIFEBOAT 8, THE FIRST lifeboat to be lowered on the port side, carried no male passengers, in accordance with Lightoller's direction. Only twenty-four first-class passengers were in it, six of whom were servants, plus four crewmen. Among those who declined to be lowered away were the thirty women and children escorted by John Hart. Although some of them got into the boat, they immediately got out again and went inside because of the cold. Hart dutifully returned below decks to fetch another third-class group.

One of the most endearing *Titanic* stories is that of Isidor and Ida Straus. When Ida was told to get into the lifeboat without her husband, she declined, saying, "No! I will not be separated from my husband. As we have lived, so we will die. Together." Someone suggested that because of Isidor's age, no one would object to him joining his wife. He reportedly replied, "No, I do not wish any distinction in my favour which is not granted to others." The elderly couple then ordered their maid, Ellen Bird, into the boat and went down to A Deck, where

The Countess of Rothes crossed the English Channel with her parents, who disembarked at Cherbourg while she remained aboard. Her actions in Lifeboat 8 made her one of the heroes of the tragedy.

they calmly sat in some deck chairs to observe the goings-on around them. Later they were seen returning to their cabin.

The women in Lifeboat 8 were unimpressed with the four crewmen in it. None of the men could row and two of them did not even realize that the oars had to be put in oarlocks before they could be used. Noel Lucy Dyer-Edwards, the Countess of Rothes, was an expert oarswoman. She gamely took charge at the tiller while other women rowed all night, initially to get away from the expected suction and then because the crewmen aboard had been told to row to a distant light, drop off their passengers, and then return to *Titanic* for more.

About this time, steward George Dodd encountered the millionaire group on A Deck waiting for the windows to be opened and directed them back up to the boat deck. Dodd thought that since all boats were being loaded there, then Lifeboat 4 would be raised back up for loading. Once again, the wealthy calmly waited while all about them lifeboats were loaded, launched, and rowed away. Time was running out.

Colliding with an iceberg at night did not upset many passengers initially. Some even picked up chunks of ice that fell off on to the deck and joked about putting them in their drinks.

CHAPTER 5

SURVIVAL

THE SECOND EIGHTY MINUTES

CONTRARY TO MOST MOVIES ABOUT *TITANIC*, there was little panic among passengers for quite a while after the ship hit the iceberg. Initially, a large number of passengers refused to leave the stricken vessel, believing that a huge ocean liner was much safer than a small lifeboat bobbing about at night on the cold North Atlantic. The realization that the ship was doomed seemed to sink in slowly, in all likelihood connected to the degree by which the bow was going under.

EMERGENCY LIFEBOAT 1 WAS LOCATED on the starboard side next to the bridge wing and was closest to the bow. It needed to be launched before the bow was too low, so the same davits could be used to launch two other lifeboats: Collapsibles C (sitting on the deck) and A (on the roof of the officers' quarters). Scandalously, it carried only a dozen people: three first-class male and two female passengers (one a servant), and seven crewmen. First Officer Murdoch had ordered five crewmen into it to pick up anyone in the water or who climbed down the falls. As it was being lowered, Sir Cosmo Duff-Gordon approached with his wife and her maid and asked if they could get into the boat. Murdoch agreed and, as there were no other passengers nearby, he put two additional crewmen into it.

The crewmen in Emergency 1 did not follow Murdoch's orders to remain near the ship but instead rowed about two hundred metres away and simply sat there for another hour and a half. No one, including the sailor in charge, lookout George Symons, or English gentleman and sportsman Duff-Gordon, seemed to want to take the responsibility to return to the ship to pick up people in the water, perhaps fearing the lifeboat would be swamped if they did so. Fashionista Lady Duff-Gordon had other things on her mind, at one stage remarking to her maid Laura Francatelli, "You have lost your beautiful nightdress." On hearing this, fireman Robert Pusey opined, "Never mind, you have saved your lives; but we have lost our kit." Sir Cosmo offered to replace the lost items and later wrote out a cheque for five pounds to each of the crewmen. This action led to accusations that he had bribed the crew not to return to pick up people in the water, a charge against which he had to defend himself at the subsequent British inquiry and for the rest of his life.

LIFEBOAT 6 WAS THE second lifeboat launched from the port side and had between twenty-four and twenty-eight people in it. It carried one male and eighteen female first-class passengers (two of them servants), a third-class male passenger, and four crew members, two of whom were women. Coincidentally, the two crewmen were lookout Fred Fleet, who had first spotted the iceberg, and quartermaster Robert Hichens, who had been at the wheel of *Titanic* when she hit the iceberg.

Montreal's Hélène Baxter made it into Lifeboat 6, carried there by her son, Quigg, as she had been suffering from sea sickness for most of the voyage. Quigg also put his married sister, Zette, and his mistress, Berthe Mayné, into the boat. When he passed his mother a silver brandy flask, she started to complain about his drinking, but he cut her off and waved goodbye to them. Quigg did not survive. Writer and lecturer Helen Candee also got into Lifeboat 6, but slipped and fell as she did so, breaking her ankle. As the lifeboat was being lowered, several women called out that there weren't enough men aboard it to row. Without any other crewmen nearby, Major Arthur Peuchen offered his services to Lightoller. When the second officer found out that Peuchen was a yachtsman, he told him to climb out on the davit to the falls and lower himself to the lifeboat, now twenty metres below. The Torontonian readily complied and got away, although

Margaret Brown was another hero of the disaster, although many of the stories about her actions in the lifeboat were pure fabrication.

he was publicly criticized later for surviving. Peuchen's friend, Harry Molson, didn't survive to be chastised. A strong swimmer, he was last seen on the deck in his stocking feet, preparing to swim to a ship whose lights he thought he saw in the distance.

A woman who was to become one of *Titanic's* best-known survivors was also in Lifeboat 6—Margaret Brown. After she had helped several other women into the lifeboat, she started looking for more. When the boat was being lowered, two of her male acquaintances picked her up and dropped her nearly a metre into it. The conventional story is that Brown essentially took command of the lifeboat from Hichens. Disillusioned, insulting, petty, and crude, Hichens resisted all entreaties to return to the foundering ship to pick up survivors still thrashing about in the water. Instead, he ordered the lifeboat's occupants to row as far and as fast as they could from the sinking ship, claiming they needed to get away from the anticipated suction. At this point, Brown supposedly went to the stern, dismissed Hichens, and took over the tiller, threatening in her best street language to throw him overboard if he moved towards her or continued to protest. Some versions of the story even have her brandishing a pistol to relieve the sulking quartermaster and actually turning the lifeboat around. But in reality it was too late to go back; by that point there was no one left alive in the water to save.

Brown did perform admirably in Lifeboat 6, sharing out her extra clothes, encouraging the women to row, and admonishing Hichens to stop his continuous gloom and doom predictions. The closest she actually came to the Molly Brown of legend was to stand up on one occasion and threaten to throw Hichens overboard—before she sat down again. Once she was rescued by *Carpathia*, Brown worked tirelessly on the rescue ship, passing out blankets and comforting others.

1:15

BY THIS POINT John Hart was once again on E Deck, trying to gather up more third-class women and children to escort to the boat deck. Most women would not leave their husbands, but he managed to convince a few of them and several single women to follow him—about twenty-five in total. At the same time, several single third-class men who had been held below decks to prevent an assumed rush on the lifeboats were released. Unfamiliar with the ship's layout, some of them climbed the well deck crane, along its boom, and dropped onto A Deck, from where they ascended one level to the boat deck.

1:20

WITH JUST AN hour left before *Titanic* went under, Lifeboat 16 was launched from the port side by Lightoller and carried between fifty and fifty-six people.

Apart from five male crewmen, they were mostly third-class women and children, as well as several stewardesses. For stewardess Violet Jessop, *Titanic* was not to be her only marine mishap. She had already been aboard *Olympic* when it collided with HMS *Hawke*. After *Titanic*, she continued to work for the White Star Line and was a nurse on *Titanic*'s sister ship, *Britannic*, when the giant vessel hit a mine in the Aegean Sea during the First World War and sank. She survived. Jessop has the distinction of having served on all three Olympic class vessels when they suffered their misfortunes.

1:25

LIFEBOAT 14 WAS lowered from the port side with sixty to sixty-three people aboard, largely a mixture of women from all three classes, as well as a number of crewmen under Fifth Officer Lowe, whom Lightoller had ordered into the boat. Most of the women left their husbands on the stricken ship. Winnipeg-bound Esther Hart—who had been having premonitions of a tragedy—and her daughter, Eva, made it into the lifeboat, but her husband, Benjamin, did not and perished. Juliette Laroche, pregnant with her third child, got in with her two daughters, Louise and Simone. Her Haitian husband, Joseph, did not survive, but Juliette delivered a son in December. Returning from their visit to Ireland, Wisconsinite Lillian Minahan and her sister-in-law, Daisy, also got in safely, but left Dr. William Minahan behind. Allegedly his last words to them were "be brave."

Benjamin Guggenheim and his valet Victor Giglio had by now returned from their cabins where they had changed into evening clothes and were sitting in the first-class smoking room, savouring drinks. When a startled Ismay asked Guggenheim why he was not trying to get into a lifeboat, the millionaire replied that they had dressed up in their best and were "prepared to go down like gentlemen." Later, he reportedly asked a steward to tell his wife that "I've done my best in doing my duty." About this time quartermaster Rowe fired his eighth and last rocket.

1:30

INITIALLY, LIFEBOAT 12 carried between thirty and forty people, including two crewmen. Since Lightoller supervised the loading, no males were allowed in it. Most of the passengers were from second class, with about five from third class. As the boat was being lowered, a third-class male jumped into it and immediately hid under the seats until it rowed safely away. Lifeboats 4 and 14 later joined up with Lifeboat 12 to transfer some passengers to it, bringing its total occupants to forty-three.

As Lifeboat 12 was being lowered on the port side, Lifeboat 9 was being lowered on the starboard one. By now, *Titanic* had a noticeable list to starboard and any lifeboats on that side in their falls were hanging away from the ship, making it difficult for female passengers to get across the gap. Murdoch stood with one foot on the deck railing and the other in the lifeboat to help them. After all immediately available women were loaded the first officer allowed any males nearby to board. Ten of them promptly complied, followed by fifteen crewmen, bringing the total to fifty-six people. Most of the passengers were from second class, along with a few from first and second. Guggenheim's mistress, Ninette Aubart, and her maid got in, along with Lily May, the wife of novelist Jacques Futrelle, but their companions remained behind. Among the males who were allowed to board was professional gambler George Brereton, travelling under the name of George Brayton, who journeyed on ocean liners first class to ply his trade. He died of a self-inflicted shotgun wound to the head in 1942. (Twenty years earlier his wife had killed herself in the same way over the death of their son following a tonsilectomy.)

1:35

BY THE TIME Lifeboat 11 was being loaded on the starboard side, almost everyone on board realized that *Titanic*'s end was near. Possibly because of this, seventy people were loaded, a mix of second and third class as well as crew. A human chain of stewards had been formed to pass women and children into the lifeboats and keep any unauthorized males back. During the confusion, Nellie Becker, her four-year-old daughter, and one-year-old son were put into the lifeboat, but twelve-year-old Ruth was left behind. Nellie was inconsolable until she found Ruth aboard *Carpathia*. Similarly, Leah Aks was separated from her ten-month-old son. As she waited to board with the baby in her arms, someone thought she was trying to jump the queue and forcibly held her back. Another person grabbed the baby and threw him into the lifeboat, where passenger Elizabeth Nye caught him. Aks could not get into the boat, but managed to clamber into another one. Aboard *Carpathia*, Nye refused to turn the baby over to Aks because she was not sure that she was his mother. Captain Rostron finally settled the issue when Aks was able to describe a birthmark on her baby.

STARBOARD SIDE LIFEBOAT 13 followed 11 by a few minutes, just one short of its sixty-five person capacity. At least thirty third-class passengers and twenty-five crew members were among its occupants, along with a smattering of first and second class passengers. One of the crewmen was Reginald Lee, the second lookout in the crow's nest when *Titanic* hit the iceberg. Murdoch let male passengers board, so Dr. Washington Dodge, teacher Lawrence Beesley, Armenian David Vartanian, and Irish piper Eugene Daly got in. Most of the third-class passengers had been brought up by steward Hart, having decided to stick it out in the cold of the lifeboat rather than the warmth inside the ship. Among the female passengers were Halifax's Hilda Slayter as well as Ruth Becker and Leah Aks, whose families were in Lifeboat 11.

As Lifeboat 13 was being lowered into the ocean, a group of third-class men jumped into it, including Irishman Daniel Buckley. Most of them were promptly dragged out, but a woman covered Buckley with her shawl and hid him. He went on to serve his new country during the First World War, but was killed by a German sniper while trying to rescue some wounded soldiers less than a month before the war ended.

As the lifeboat got nearer the water, some of its occupants noticed a huge rush of water shooting out the side of the ship directly below them. It was discharge from pumps attempting to pump water from below decks, which would have swamped the lifeboat. Some passengers shouted to the deck hands to stop lowering the boat, while crewmen pushed it away from *Titanic's* side with their oars until the boat was safely past the discharge. Meanwhile, Lifeboat 13 had drifted backwards towards the ship and was now directly beneath Lifeboat 11. More shouts to the deck above stopped the lowering of Lifeboat 11 until Lifeboat 13 was able to row away.

Teacher Lawrence Beesley, centre, pictured with some of his students, wrote one of the first books about the disaster.

Lifeboat 15 was the last standard one lowered from the starboard side and was overloaded with seventy people. There were about forty third-class passengers, divided almost evenly between men and women and including six children, a first-class passenger, as well as twenty-six crew members, one of them female. The occupants included most of the women and children John Hart had brought up from below on his two trips. He was on his way down for another group when Murdoch ordered him into the lifeboat. In total, the gallant steward saved fifty-eight third-class passengers, one-third of all third-class passengers saved.

1:45

EMERGENCY 2, THE forward boat on the port side, was lowered with about twenty-six people in it. By now, the sea had climbed over the top of the bow and *Titanic* had a significant list to port. Lightoller was in a hurry to launch Emergency 2 because he needed to use its davits for Collapsible D, which was stored on the deck beside it. Most of its occupants were women and children from first and third class, plus a third-class male who jumped in as the boat was being lowered with his wife and daughter aboard. There were also three crewmen under Fourth Officer Boxhall, who had been ordered into it by Lightoller. Before this loading occurred, at least twenty-five crewmen had gotten into the boat, only to be told "Get out of there you damned cowards! I'd like to see every one of you overboard!" by Lightoller, who carried a pistol in his hand. The men meekly obeyed.

1:50

LIFEBOAT 4 WAS the second-last standard lifeboat to be lowered, although originally it was going to be the first. It had been forgotten about after no one could find the special tool to open the windows on A deck and it was left hanging in its falls, outside the windows. Meanwhile, several millionaires had been waiting patiently to board it, first on A deck and now on the boat deck where steward George Dodd had sent them. After launching Emergency 2, Lightoller discovered that Lifeboat 4 had not been launched and its intended occupants were now waiting on the boat deck. He promptly directed them back down to A deck, as the required tool had been found. By now, the list to port had caused Lifeboat 4 to swing too far away for easy access, so grappling hooks were used to pull it closer, while a small ladder allowed the women and children to climb out the window and into the boat.

Helped by her husband and accompanied by her maid and nurse, Madeleine Astor was the first person to enter Lifeboat 4. When Astor asked Lightoller if he might join his wife because of her "delicate condition," the dogmatic officer refused. The millionaire then stepped back and helped other women through the window. Other men who remained on deck besides Astor while their wives, children, and female servants got in the lifeboat included John Thayer, George Widener, Arthur Ryerson, and William Carter. Once the latter saw his wife, son, and daughter safely into the lifeboat, he quickly scuttled across to the starboard side in search of another lifeboat. Before the lifeboat was lowered to the water, by now only one deck below, the remaining men were offered seats. None of them accepted. Because there were no sailors in the lifeboat, two crewmen were ordered to slide down the falls into the boat, bringing the total to four. As the boat was rowed away, its occupants could see Astor, Ryerson, John Thayer and son Jack, and George Widener and son Harry waving to them.

Quartermaster Walter Perkis, who had just slid down the falls, was in charge of the lifeboat and had orders to row to the aft gangway to pick up more passengers. On the way, he managed to pull seven crewmen from the water, two of whom would died of exposure; one in the lifeboat and one aboard *Carpathia*. There were now about forty people in the lifeboat. Back on *Titanic*, Astor, probably assisted by his servant, went below decks and released the dogs from their kennels, including his Airedale, Kitty. Madeleine later reported that she could see Kitty running around the boat deck as *Titanic* went under. Two lapdogs survived the sinking, carried into lifeboats by their owners.

1:55

BECAUSE OF LIGHTOLLER's direction, Lifeboat 10 left without any male passengers in it and carried forty-eight women and children from all three classes, plus seven crewmen. It was the last standard lifeboat to leave the port side and was lowered shortly after Lifeboat 4. Most women in it left a man standing on the deck. Winnipegger Mary Fortune got away with her three daughters, but left husband Mark and son Charles behind. Montreal-bound passengers Antoinine Mallet, who escaped with her infant son, and Mathilde Weisz, left their husbands on the ship. Emile Richard, the family friend travelling with the Mallets, also

Women assist Titanic's *sailors to row a lifeboat as* Carpathia *approaches on the horizon.*

remained on the ship. Similarly, Ettie Dean got separated from husband Bertram, but escaped with her infant children, Bert and Millvina. Millvina died on May 31, 2009, the last of *Titanic*'s survivors. Chief baker Charles Joughin was assigned to Lifeboat 10, but he was so engrossed in loading children—literally throwing them into the boat—that he failed to get in himself. One person who did not miss the boat was Armenian Neshan Krekorian, who was travelling with five of his countrymen to Brantford, Ontario. As the lifeboat was being lowered past A Deck, he jumped into it and survived, although he caught pneumonia and had to be hospitalized in New York.

2:00

BY NOW, ONLY the four collapsibles remained to be launched. Collapsible C was the first, lowered on the starboard side from the same davits as Lifeboat 1. All of its forty passengers but two were from third class, and most of them were women. There were also six crewmen aboard. As the lifeboat was being loaded, quartermaster George Rowe asked for more women and children. When none stepped forward immediately, some men waiting nearby moved towards the lifeboat, only to be stopped by Chief Purser Hugh McElroy, who fired two warning shots into the air.

A majority of the passengers in Collapsible C were from Syrian Lebanon, including Canada-bound Mariana Assaf, as well as brother and sister Jamila and Elias Nicola-Yarred. The youngsters ended up briefly in Liverpool, Nova Scotia, where an uncle ran a store, before being reunited with their parents in Florida. Because of *Titanic*'s list to port, Collapsible C had to be held away from the ship's side to prevent the rivets from damaging its canvas sides. As the lifeboat was being lowered, J. Bruce Ismay and William Carter stepped into it. One can only imagine what thoughts flashed through the minds of men like Chief Officer Wilde, First Officer Murdoch, and Chief Purser McElroy as they observed the chairman of their company save himself on one of the last available lifeboats while they were doomed to die.

Under quartermaster Rowe the crew rowed all night towards a light they thought they saw in the distance and by daylight were eight kilometres away from *Titanic*. During the night, five Chinese sailors were discovered under the seats, part of a group of eight travelling third class to New York to their next ship. Having a good idea of their chances of getting into a lifeboat legitimately, they realized their best hope was to stow away in the collapsible.

BY NOW, THERE were only fifteen minutes left before *Titanic* slipped away forever. Collapsible D was hooked into the davits where Lifeboat 2 had been. It was launched with forty people in it, about ten under capacity. To prevent anyone from storming the boat, crewmen formed a human chain and allowed only women and children through. Irene Harris, who had been warned by a male stranger to get off at Cherbourg, should have taken his advice. She got into the collapsible, but her husband remained behind and died. New Yorker William Hoyt passed his wife through to the lifeboat, and then jumped into the ocean where he thought it would end up. His stratagem worked, and he was pulled shivering from the water. Passengers Hugh Woolner and Mauritz Bjornstrom-Steffanson had a similar idea. They had been helping to load other passengers into lifeboats and decided it was now time to try and get away, especially since water was lapping around their feet. As they stood on the railing preparing to dive, they noticed Collapsible D being lowered into the water just below them. They jumped. Bjornstrom-Steffanson landed on his head in the bow, while Woolner almost missed the boat and ended up hanging over its side. He was hauled in as the lifeboat reached the water.

Captain Smith entered the wireless room and released the two operators, Phillips and Bride, from their duties. After he left, the two Marconi employees remained at their post for another twelve minutes while Phillips sent *Titanic*'s last transmission. As he returned to the bridge, Smith told any of his crewmen that he encountered that it was "every man for himself." By now, *Titanic*'s stern was completely out of the water and her giant propellers were visible.

BAND LEADER WALLACE HARTLEY and three of his musicians began to play their last piece. Debate continues to this day as to what it was. At about the same time, *Titanic*'s designer Thomas Andrews sat alone in the first-class smoking room, deep in thought. His arms were folded across his chest and his lifebelt was on the table beside him.

THE ONLY TWO LIFEBOATS left now were Collapsibles B and A, lashed to the port and starboard sides respectively of the roof of the officers' quarters. Several

Thomas Andrews knew before anyone else how long Titanic *would survive. He chose to go down with his creation.*

men pushed Collapsible B onto the boat deck, where it landed upside down. While they struggled to right it, a wave lifted the lifeboat off the deck, over the railing, and into the frigid sea, along with First Officer Lightoller, Sixth Officer Moody, and dozens of others. In all likelihood, this wave also drowned Captain Smith, who had been standing on the port side of the bridge wing. As people tried to climb onto the still upside down collapsible, the stabilizing guy wires holding the ship's forward funnel snapped and the smokestack toppled over, killing several swimmers. Some sources maintain that John Jacob Astor was one of them.

Although the funnel missed Collapsible B, the wave it caused when it hit the water washed everyone off the lifeboat and pushed it about twenty metres farther away. At the same time, First Officer Lightoller and Colonel Archibald Gracie were sucked against the gratings of some blowers and held there by water pouring through the blower openings to the decks below. Unable to extricate themselves, they were only saved when a huge blast of air displaced by the water blew them free. They managed to crawl onto Collapsible B, where they joined wireless operators Harold Bride and Jack Phillips, baker Charles Joughin, young Jack Thayer, and several others. James Moody, the most junior of the ship's officers, was not among them.

The situation on overturned Collapsible B was desperate. Everyone on it had been in the frigid water and all were soaked through. Initially, there were about

Until 1985 most people believed that Titanic *went down in one piece instead of two.*

"The starlight night was beautiful"

Stern
2nd class
Section of ship

Every porthole
& saloon was
blazing with light"

"We had sixty
or seventy
on board"

Archibald Gracie experienced one of the most amazing survivals of the entire disaster.

three dozen people on the collapsible and as more tried to clamber aboard, they were turned away to prevent overloading. To counter the slight swell that developed and in an attempt to keep the boat from tipping, everyone stood and followed Lightoller's directions of "Lean to the left, lean to the right." Several men died during the night and slipped into the water, including Phillips.

Collapsible A was also pushed off the roof of the officers' quarters, but fortunately it landed upright on the boat deck. The wave that floated off Collapsible B did the same to Collapsible A, along with the men standing around it. A few were already in the lifeboat when this happened, and were quickly joined by several others who climbed aboard out of the freezing sea. Then, the same wave caused by the forward funnel falling hit Collapsible A, washing everyone away and filing the lifeboat with water as its collapsible canvas sides were still down. In the ocean, several more people managed to scramble into the boat and, once aboard, helped others into it. During the night, at least a dozen men died and all but three of their bodies were dropped overboard.

Titanic's stern continued to rise higher, causing all loose items and several fixed ones inside the ship—including boilers, engines, and coal—to slide towards the bow. Anyone still aboard had to grasp something to keep from being swept along. Father Thomas Byles was on the after well deck, surrounded by about a hundred Catholics, hearing their confessions till the very end. Down in the ship's bowels, the entire thirty-five man engineering crew, who had been fighting to maintain power to keep the lights on, went down with the ship.

2:20

ALL *TITANIC* MOVIES made before the discovery of the wreck on the ocean floor in 1985 showed the ship going down by the bow until the stern eventually

One of Titanic's *lifeboats, photographed from* Carpathia.

rose out of the water and *Titanic* slipped straight under to her watery grave. In fact, a large portion of the after part of the vessel—between the third and fourth funnels—broke nearly free, but remained attached at the keel. It floated briefly by itself before the forward part pulled it into a vertical position and then down to the bottom. Despite the fact that many survivors had reported this, movies continued to show *Titanic* going down in one piece, until the incontrovertible evidence of the discovery of the wreck proved otherwise.

IN THE WATER

BY THE TIME *Titanic* went under, there were well over a thousand people in the ice-cold North Atlantic, struggling desperately to stay alive. Their struggles did not last long. When exposed to continuous cold, body heat is lost. If the body's internal mechanisms cannot replenish that lost heat, then a drop in core body temperature occurs. Hypothermia sets in when the core body temperature drops below 35°C—the temperature required for normal metabolism and body functions. Once body temperature starts to decrease various symptoms appear, beginning with shivering as the body tries to generate more heat. Impairment of cognitive functioning and judgement occurs, followed by disorientation, unconsciousness, and death. Heat is lost more quickly in water than on land as cold water carries heat away from the body twenty-five times faster than air of the same temperature. Water temperatures around freezing can lead to unconsciousness in as little as fifteen minutes and death within forty-five minutes, although individual response varies depending on such factors as clothing (including life vests), body fat, age, and activity.

Ruth Becker, the twelve-year-old who escaped in Lifeboat 13 and met up with her mother and two siblings aboard *Carpathia*, remembered the sounds that echoed across the dark water: "There fell on the ear the most terrible noises that human beings ever listened to—the cries of hundreds of people struggling in the icy cold water, crying for help with a cry that we knew could not be answered." Reluctant to talk about the tragedy until old age, when Ruth died in 1990 her ashes were scattered over the spot where *Titanic* lies on the ocean floor.

Seven-year-old Winnipeg-bound Eva Hart had similar memories. Safely in Lifeboat 14 with her mother, Eva recalled "the ghastly noise of the people thrashing about and screaming and drowning, that finally ceased. I remember saying to my mother once, 'How dreadful that noise was' and I'll always remember her reply 'yes, but think back about the silence that followed it.'"

A Titanic lifeboat, photographed from Carpathia.

CHAPTER 6

RESCUE—AND RECOVERY

IN THE LIFEBOATS

AFTER *TITANIC* WENT DOWN and the last of the cries died out, there were just over seven hundred people bobbing around in twenty lifeboats in the middle of a vast, empty, dark, and cold expanse of ocean, shared only with dozens of icebergs. Many survivors were inadequately dressed against the biting cold and several were soaked through. Contrary to regulations, the lifeboats were not equipped with any form of emergency equipment, although one had a lantern. Except for Lightoller and Bride trying to stay balanced on overturned Collapsible B, no one knew that *Carpathia* was on the way. Fourth Officer Boxhall began

Titanic *survivors aboard the rescue ship* Carpathia.

firing off a box of small green flares that he had brought into Emergency 2 with him, in the hope that people in other lifeboats would see them and row towards him. At 2:30 A.M. *Carpathia* spotted one of the flares in the far distance and, in response thirty minutes later, Captain Rostron ordered a rocket fired every fifteen minutes.

Although the lifeboats were fairly scattered, several of them joined together and transferred passengers to balance loads. Despite the enormity of the disaster, petty arguments broke out in some boats over the most mundane things, such as crewmen smoking in the presence of women. Sadly, only one lifeboat went back in an attempt to pull people out of the water. After he transferred people between four other boats—not without some difficulty—Fifth Officer Lowe set off to find survivors at about three o'clock. There weren't many. In the end, Lowe recovered only four people, one of whom soon died. One who lived was Japanese passenger Masabumi Hosono, who had tied himself to a door. He was hauled into the lifeboat nearly dead, but soon warmed up and rowed for the rest of the night. Hosono was ostracized in Japan for having survived.

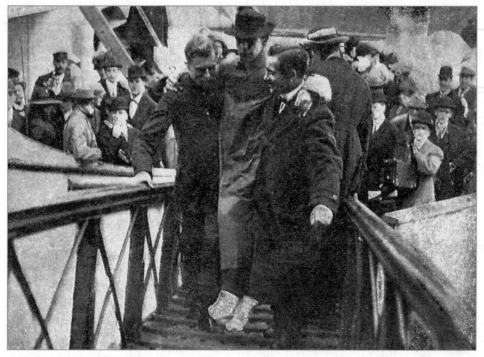

Radio operator Harold Bride is carried off Carpathia *at New York. He suffered frostbite to his feet from being in the water.*

RESCUE

SURVIVORS FIRST SPOTTED one of *Carpathia*'s rockets at 3:30 and forty minutes later the first women started to climb ladders up the rescue ship's side. *Carpathia* moved slowly through the scattered lifeboats, picking up their grateful occupants, at the same time as more distant boats started to row towards the rescue ship. By 8:45 all lifeboats had been unloaded and the survivors were being cared for, with hot drinks, food, and blankets. With full daylight, Captain Rostron steamed slowly through the whole area, searching for more survivors. There were no more, although there was lots of wreckage and—according to Rostron—only one body, which he left in the ocean. *Carpathia* did not have enough supplies to continue her eastward journey, so Rostron decided to return to New York. Before he left, he had thirteen of *Titanic*'s lifeboats winched aboard, leaving three lifeboats and all four collapsibles in the water. Collapsible A still had three bod-ies in it. As *Carpathia* was about to depart, two other ships appeared, *Mount Temple* and *Californian*. Rostron asked their captains to continue searching, but neither found any survivors—or bodies.

The wreck of the ss Atlantic *off Prospect, Nova Scotia, caused 562 deaths. All married men, all women, and all but one child perished.*

At 4:00 P.M., Rostron stopped his ship, conducted a brief religious service in the main lounge, and buried four people—one who was brought aboard already dead and three who died after rescue. The survivors on *Carpathia* collected fifteen thousand dollars for the crew to thank them for their rescue efforts. The Cunard Line refused to let its employees keep the money and instead turned it over to charities for the survivors. Cunard also refused to accept money from the White Star Line for any expenses incurred in the rescue, although out of its own funds Cunard paid *Carpathia*'s crew an extra month's wages. White Star, on the other hand, stopped paying *Titanic*'s surviving crew members as of the minute of their ship's sinking, and never gave them anything for their distress and suffering. The same survivors' committee that collected the money later presented Rostron with a loving cup.

Shortly after 9:00 P.M. on April 18, *Carpathia* entered New York harbour, steamed past the Cunard pier, and stopped further on at White Star's pier, where Rostron had *Titanic*'s lifeboats unloaded. *Carpathia* then returned to the Cunard pier, where around thirty thousand people were waiting. In recognition of the disaster, normal immigration regulations were suspended, which would have included a stop at Ellis Island. Propriety was still observed: first- and second-class

The Reverend William Ancient organized the burials of the victims of the ss Atlantic *disaster.*

passengers disembarked first, and when they were all off by 10:30, third-class passengers followed. In anticipation of a formal inquiry, all of *Titanic*'s crew were held on another ship until they were no longer needed. The rescue operation was complete; now the grisly task of recovery would commence.

SS *ATLANTIC*

FOR MANY YEARS, when ships foundered and people were killed, the normal procedure was for passing ships to bury at sea any bodies that they found, unless the shipwreck occurred close to shore. In that instance, local civilian or military authorities assumed responsibility for the recovery of any bodies and their subsequent burial on land. That had been the case in 1873, when the ss *Atlantic* foundered off Prospect, Nova Scotia. The 3,707-ton *Atlantic* had been constructed for the White Star Line by Harland and Wolff in 1870. On the night of April 1, she struck an underwater rock with the loss of 562 passengers and crew of 932 aboard. The White Star Line's first tragedy at sea was also the greatest transatlantic passenger ship disaster of the nineteenth century. Subsequently the sinking of *Titanic* became the largest similar disaster of the twentieth century.

In the *Atlantic* catastrophe, Reverend William Johnson Ancient, the local minister who organized the rescue operation, also took charge of the burial arrangements. In all, 427 bodies were buried locally over a six-week period in two long pits, 277 in the graveyard of the Anglican church near Sandy Cove for Protestants, and 150 in the Roman Catholic Star of the Sea Cemetery at Prospect. Mothers and their young children were buried together where possible, while some coffins contained up to three corpses. Coffins were stacked four deep and trenches lengthened for additional bodies.

PASSING SHIPS

AS *CARPATHIA* DOCKED at New York City, 1,550 kilometres to the east, several lifeless bodies—the exact number will never be known—that went down with *Titanic* on her descent to the bottom of the ocean were now entombed in the ship for all eternity. Hundreds of other bodies—again, the exact number will never be known—floated in the cold North Atlantic. Many corpses were swept away by the currents to simply disappear. A large number continued to bob about on the ocean over or near the spot where *Titanic* went under. Some were seen by passing ships, although most steamed many kilometres out of the way of the disaster area to avoid the ghastly sight.

One of the ships that passed through *Titanic*'s debris field was the German liner ss *Bremen*, which sighted wreckage and bodies on April 20 while sailing from Bremen to New York. Passengers and crew reported seeing more than a hundred corpses floating in the water, along with deck chairs, pieces of wood, an upside-down lifeboat, and other flotsam.

The experiences of the men and women aboard the *Bremen* are some of the earliest descriptions of *Titanic*'s victims and remain among the most vivid of all accounts. Although the ship's officers were reluctant to talk about what they had seen, several of the passengers were not as reticent. One of the first-class passengers, Mrs. Johanna Stunke, told reporters in New York:

> *It was between four and five o'clock, Saturday, April 20th, when our ship sighted an iceberg off the bow to starboard. As we drew nearer, and could make out small dots floating around in the sea, a feeling of awe and sadness crept over everyone on the ship. We passed within a hundred feet of the southernmost drift of the wreckage, and looking down over the rail we distinctly saw a number of bodies so clearly that we could make out what they were wearing and whether they*

were men or women. We saw one woman in her night dress, with a baby clasped closely to her breast. There was another woman, fully dressed, with her arms tight around the body of a shaggy dog. The bodies of three men in a group, all clinging to one steamship chair, floated nearby, and just beyond them were a dozen bodies of men, all of them encased in life-preservers, clinging together as though in a last desperate struggle for life...those were the only bodies we passed near enough to distinguish, but we could see the white life-preservers of many more dotting the sea, all the way to the iceberg. The officers told us that was probably the berg hit by the Titanic, and that the bodies and ice had drifted along together.

Although a number of passengers demanded that *Bremen*'s captain stop and pick up the bodies, the officers assured them that they had just received a wireless message stating that a ship dispatched expressly to recover bodies was only two hours away. That vessel was a cable ship contracted by White Star Line officials after they realized that they had to do something in an attempt to recover as many *Titanic* victims as possible to protect their reputation. As an initial step, they chartered *Mackay-Bennett*, the first of four ships to sail from Halifax to undertake this gruesome task.

CS *MACKAY-BENNETT*

GIVEN THE LOCATION of the *Titanic* sinking, either St. John's, Newfoundland, or Halifax, Nova Scotia, was a suitable port from which to mount the recovery operation. Both were situated on the edge of the main North Atlantic shipping lines and had adequate facilities to handle the task. While Halifax's services were better, St. John's was closer to the sinking and ships could get to the site quicker. In the end, however, Halifax was selected because of its mainland rail connections to the rest of North America. If relatives requested it, this would make the shipping of remains to any location on the continent a simpler task than trying to send them from Newfoundland.

A. G. Jones and Company represented the White Star Line in Halifax as its authorized agent. During the evening of April 16, the company chartered a ship to recover as many bodies as possible, based on direction received from White Star officials. The vessel selected was the steam-driven CS (Cable Ship) *Mackay-Bennett* owned by the Commercial Cable Company under the command of

The Cable Ship Mackay-Bennett *undergoes maintenance in dry dock at Halifax.*

Captain Frederick Harold Larnder (frequently misspelled Lardner) of Halifax. Normally used to lay and repair the company's transatlantic undersea telegraph cables, she was chartered at a rate of $550 U.S. per day. Only crewmen who had volunteered for "work that was unsettling" were allowed to sail on the recovery mission. Initially, it was felt that only one ship would be necessary to recover any remains. Many experts thought there would be few, if any, bodies to recover, as they believed that most people would have been sucked down in a great vortex as the ship sank, or were trapped inside the wreckage. Even as these theories were being expressed publicly by several learned men, reports arrived of ships passing through a huge field of floating debris—and bodies.

Although registered in London, England, *Mackay-Bennett* (pronounced "Mackie-Bennett") spent much of her time operating out of Halifax repairing transatlantic undersea cables. She also worked frequently on the European side of the Atlantic, where Plymouth, England, was her home port. *Mackay-Bennett* had been built in Glasgow, Scotland, by John Elder and Company and launched in September 1884. The 79-metre long cable ship had a registered tonnage of

Mackay-Bennett *lays cable off the coast.*

1,731 tons. It was named after the two men who formed the Commercial Cable Company, John Mackay and James Bennett.

THE DEATH SHIP

PREPARATIONS FOR THE ship's grim task began immediately. Jones hired the Halifax firm of John Snow and Company Limited—the largest such firm in Nova Scotia—to prepare any bodies recovered from the ocean for burial. The company's chief embalmer, John R. Snow, Jr., had 125 rough-hewn coffins and all the embalming fluid in the city (sufficient for 70 persons) put on board, along with several pounds of ice to help preserve bodies being taken to Halifax. Canvas to wrap bodies in and scrap iron to weigh them down were also included for any that would be buried at sea. Canon Kenneth Cameron Hind, the priest's assistant at the city's Anglican Cathedral Church of All Saints, went aboard to conduct burial services at sea.

Mackay-Bennett—already termed the "Death Ship" by several newspapers—sailed from her wharf at Upper Water Street at 12:28 P.M. on Wednesday, April 17, two days after *Titanic* went down. She arrived at the reported site of the disaster on the evening of April 20, having sailed thirteen hundred kilometres. By then, it was too late to start the gruesome task of recovering the bodies; that began the next morning. It soon became apparent that there were many more bodies floating on the ocean than had been expected. According to Captain Larnder, the sight was "like nothing so much as a flock of sea gulls resting upon the water...All we could see at first would be the top of the life preservers." The lifebelts had kept the bodies upright so that "they were all floating face upwards, apparently standing in the water."

Lookouts on *Mackay-Bennett*'s bridge and bow scanned the sea for bodies. When some were seen, two or more of the ship's cutters, each with a few crewmen, were lowered over the side. Recovering the remains was a grim job. To prevent the small boats from overturning, some sailors would move to one side while others used hooks to grab the bodies and bring them closer to the rowboat. Once alongside, the cold, wet, heavy bodies had to be manhandled aboard. After a few bodies, usually four to nine depending on sea conditions, were recovered, the cutter returned to the mother ship to unload them. Then the sailors went back to their grisly task, repeating it several times in the course of a day—as long as the weather held. If additional bodies were spotted while the cutters were already over the side, the crewmen were directed to them by flags and whistles

Horses were stabled and hearses stored at the carriage house of Snow's Undertakers.

from *Mackay-Bennett*. At the end of the day, when there was insufficient light to collect more bodies, markers were put on any bodies floating nearby so they could be easily spotted the next day.

Once a body came aboard *Mackay-Bennett*, a set course of action was followed. A numbered tag was tied to the body, and the same number was put on a small canvas bag. Then the undertakers and their assistants examined the body, its clothing, and personal effects in detail and recorded this information on a card. In most cases, victims' ages were overestimated due to the effects of water, sun, and marine life on the body. Personal effects were put in the canvas bags, although occasionally, a ring, religious medallion, or rosary was left on the body. With the examination complete, a decision then had to be made for each corpse: burial at sea or transport to Halifax?

CLASSED IN DEATH

TODAY, IT IS NOT known what detailed instructions, if any, were given to Captain Larnder and John Snow with regard to burial at sea as opposed to return to Halifax for any recovered bodies. In any case, as implements for both options were carried aboard the ship, it is obvious that discussions had occurred before *Mackay-Bennett*'s departure about these possibilities. Given the lack of any

The White Star Line contracted Snow and Company Undertakers to make all burial arrangements. John Snow, Jr., the son of the firm's founder, sailed on two recovery ships.

records containing the reasons for burial at sea or return to Halifax, it appears that the decisions may have been based largely on three criteria: positive identification of the remains, their physical condition, and (perhaps to a lesser degree), whether the individual was a member of the crew or a passenger. If a passenger, whether first, second, or third class also seems to have had a bearing on this decision. Bodies to be taken to Halifax were then embalmed, until the embalming fluid ran out.

One of the more persistent myths about the class distinction of the time was that only first-class passengers were put into coffins at sea. *Mackay-Bennett* carried 125 coffins, yet the bodies of just 29 first-class males were taken to Halifax, leaving 96 coffins for others. Given the standards of the times, those aboard the ship may have felt uncomfortable with the bodies of women and children covered only by canvas, so they were likely put into coffins as well. This left coffins for some of the remaining bodies of adult males, whether passengers or crew. With all 125 coffins used, there remained 65 bodies to be taken to Halifax that required some other means of covering. Bodies buried at sea had used most of the canvas, leaving some victims to be covered as a group with tarpaulins rather than sewn individually into shrouds. Additionally, even if enough canvas had been available, it is highly unlikely that there was enough time for *Mackay-Bennett's* crew to sew all the bodies into shrouds before the ship returned to Halifax.

COMMITTED TO THE DEEP

BODY NO. 6, recovered on April 21, was the first one buried at sea. The unknown male, whose age was estimated at twenty-two, had black hair. His right hand had a blue tattoo mark with a copper wire ring on the thumb. He was wearing a blue serge coat and vest, black pants, a blue and white checked shirt, and black boots without socks. Burials at sea were conducted in the evenings by Captain Larnder and Canon Hind. Chief electrician Frederic Hamilton recorded the scene in his diary:

> *The tolling of the bell summoned all hands to the forecastle where thirty bodies are to be committed to the deep, each carefully weighted and carefully sewn up in canvas. It is a weird scene, this gathering. The crescent moon is shedding a faint light on us, as the ship lays wallowing in the great rollers...for nearly an hour the words "For as much as it hath pleased...we therefore commit his body to the deep" are repeated and at each interval comes, splash! as the weighted body plunges into the sea, there to sink to a depth of about two miles. Splash, splash, splash.*

Over the following five days, 86 more burials would be conducted from *Mackay-Bennett*, many of the bodies nameless. In hindsight, it seems that a little

John Snow, Jr. (left), stands beside stacked coffins ready to be loaded aboard ship to recover victims of the Titanic *disaster.*

more investigation on the part of responsible authorities could have identified more of these anonymous victims. For example, Body No. 36, which remained unknown, had several items that should have led to his identification, if only they had been published in Southampton or other newspapers. The dark-haired male, had on a steward's uniform and first-class steward's badge No. 76. His body had numerous tattoos: covering his left arm, clasped hands and a heart on his right forearm, and Japanese fans on his breast. Among his personal effects were a gold ring on the right little finger, engraved "Madge," a gold watch and chain, a seal, a silver matchbox, keys, wine cards, and a gold brooch.

The first identified victim to be buried at sea was Body No. 14, which was readily ascertained from the third-class ticket found on him as Leslie Williams, a Welsh blacksmith and professional bantamweight boxer. Williams was on his way to the United States in the company of fellow Welsh boxer, David Bowen, on a twelve-month contract for a series of boxing matches. Bowen's body was never found. The two men had originally booked on *Lusitania*, but at the last minute Williams was unable to embark on the day. Although it was announced in newspapers that Williams would be buried in New York in accordance with his wife's wishes, he had already been buried at sea.

MORE BODIES

THE BODY OF first-class passenger Frederick Sutton was the forty-sixth recovered. Sutton was originally from England but lived in Haddonfield, New Jersey, across the river from Philadelphia. He was a property developer and ran a coffee import business. A friend of Sutton's travelled to Halifax to retrieve the corpse, which had been erroneously reported as being brought to the port city in the *Camden Post-Telegraph*, when Sutton had already been buried at sea.

In the same article, it was also reported that the body of fellow Philadelphian George Widener had been recovered and buried at sea. The newspaper story was based on a message from *Mackay-Bennett* stating that the body of "G. Widen" had been found and Philadelphia newspapers speculated that it was George. In fact, neither the body of George, nor of his son, Harry, was recovered. Nevertheless, Widener's brother—thinking the report was correct and that his brother had been buried at sea—went to Halifax in the hope that Harry's body would be one of those brought into port. Aboard *Titanic*, George and Harry had helped Eleanor—George's wife—and her maid, Amalie Gieger, into Lifeboat 4 and then calmly stepped back. Body No. 45 was Edwin Keeping, George Widener's valet.

Eleanor Widener (left) survived, but her husband, George (right), perished, along with their son Harry.

Edwin was easily identified from his personal belongings, including a locket he had been given by a Russian grand duke for whom he had once worked. Eleanor later started a trust fund for Keeping's widow and his three-year-old daughter and devoted the rest of her life to charitable work.

While some bodies buried at sea remained anonymous initially, they were identified afterwards from their personal effects. For example, later that year Body No. 31 was identified from an envelope found on it (addressed to Mrs. Evans in Southampton) as William Evans, a coal trimmer. Similarly, second-class passenger Joseph Nicholls (Body No. 101) was buried at sea as unknown. He was identified later from his effects by two brothers from Michigan who had travelled to Halifax to claim the body of a third brother who died in the sinking and who knew Nicholls. Other remains took longer to identify, some several years later. Body No. 28 was not identified until 1991 as Joseph Caram, one of a group of Syrian Lebanese travelling together to Ottawa.

On day 2—Monday, April 22—twenty-six bodies were recovered, of which fifteen were buried at sea. Among them was eleven-year-old Will Sage (Body No. 67), who was travelling with his father, mother, and eight siblings from England to Florida. The entire family perished in the disaster, and Will's body was the only one found.

Body No. 73 was not initially identified, but became known a few days later from a pocket handkerchief marked "H. J." as that of third assistant electrical engineer Herbert Jupe. In May, a letter was received in Halifax from Jupe's father, asking for the return of his son's silver watch and handkerchief, which "He bought him a half doz of the same when he was at Belfast..." The heart-wrenching letter went on to state, "we are extremely obliged for all your kindness to my precious Boy He was not married and was the Love of our Hearts and he loved his Home But God gave and God has taken him Blessed be the Name of the Lord. He has left an Aceing [aching] Void in our Home which cannot be filled." Herbert's effects were sent to his parents.

On day 3—Tuesday, April 23—although 128 bodies (Nos. 78-206) were recovered, none were buried at sea as the amount of canvas for shrouds was too low. A wireless message requesting additional canvas resulted in the passing Allan Line liner *Sardinian* providing all the canvas she had aboard at 7:00 P.M. This allowed the crew to bury seventy-seven bodies at sea on April 24, the last day on which burials occurred. In all, 116 bodies were buried from *Mackay-Bennett*. Among the last remains buried at sea was Body No. 181, Ottawa journalist Mansour Novel, a naturalized Canadian of Lebanese origin who was travelling third class. Novel had left his family in Lebanon, at the time a part of Syria. When he was found, he was wearing five shirts, perhaps put on in an attempt to combat the expected cold water.

Another of the last passengers buried at sea was Rossmore Abbott (Body No. 190). The sixteen-year-old boy had embarked at Southampton with his mother, Rhoda (mistakenly listed as Rosa in the passenger manifest), and fourteen-year-old brother, Eugene. Originally from England, Rhoda had emigrated to Rhode Island, where she met and married Stanton Abbott, another Briton who became middleweight boxing champion of the United States. When they separated in 1911 she returned to England with her sons aboard *Olympic* to start a new life. When Rossmore and Eugene became homesick for their friends in the United States, Rhoda decided to return. The family was not initially booked on *Titanic*, but were delighted to be redirected to the new ship due to the coal strike.

Sleeping in their third-class cabin, the Abbotts were not awoken by a steward until 12:15 A.M.—some time after the collision. When they made it to the deck, Rhoda refused to leave her sons—considered adults at the time—to get into one of the last remaining lifeboats, Collapsible C. As the ship made its final plunge, the Abbotts were on the poop deck and were pulled under by the limited suction

HARVARD UNIVERSITY SWIM TEST

Eleanor Widener donated $2 million to build a library at Harvard in memory of her son, who had graduated from that university in 1907. The Harry Elkins Widener Memorial Library opened in 1915. A legend associated with her donation stated that she had stipulated that each graduate of the university had to pass a swimming test, supposedly because she felt that her son might have survived if he had been able to swim. Although for several years it was a requirement to pass a swim test to graduate, this regulation has nothing to do with Widener's bequest and actually dates from the 1920s. In any case, even if Harry had been the best swimmer in the world, it is unlikely he would have survived long enough in the freezing water to swim to a lifeboat.

---

that resulted. When Rhoda came back to the surface, she could not find her sons among the struggling bodies.

Just as she felt all was lost, a strong arm hauled her into Collapsible A, giving Rhoda the distinction of being the only woman aboard *Titanic* to survive after being in the water; all other female survivors boarded lifeboats. As its sides had not been raised, the twenty or so occupants of Collapsible A were forced to stand in icy water up to their knees until rescued. Only thirteen survived the ordeal—including Rhoda. As an occupant died, his body was usually thrown overboard to lighten the load and create more space for the living. Eugene's body was never found.

The very last remains buried at sea from *Mackay-Bennett* were those of John Davies (Body No. 200), who went by the odd title of extra second baker aboard *Titanic*. By the time Davies's body was buried, many people who had had relatives or friends aboard *Titanic* were upset about the large number of burials at sea and were demanding that more bodies be brought into port for proper identification and burial. Whether this had any effect or not is unknown, but none of the 106 bodies recovered by *Mackay-Bennett* after Davies were buried at sea.

Despite the recovery ship's meticulous record-keeping, some errors did occur. For example, Body No. 151 was James Robinson, a saloon steward. Initially, it was reported that his remains were taken to Halifax, while a later (and correct) report states he was buried at sea. Another potential error concerned Hugh

McElroy, *Titanic*'s chief purser. When Body No. 157 was first examined, it was listed as D. Lily, steward. A review of the ship's roster in Halifax revealed that there was no D. Lily and the body was noted as unidentified. The address of a Miss McElroy found among the effects pointed to the identity of the chief purser, but the description of his uniform did not seem to mark a man of his rank and importance aboard the ship. Was another error made?

On day 5—Thursday, April 25—eighty-seven more bodies were found and taken on board (Nos. 206–292). The next day, a second chartered ship arrived from Halifax to take over *Mackay-Bennett*'s duties. In the pre-dawn hours, CS *Minia* drifted within sight of her sister cable ship until it was light enough to commence work. The *Minia* crew then transferred embalming fluid across to *Mackay-Bennett* before the two searched together. *Mackay-Bennett* recovered fourteen more bodies (Nos. 293–306) before she departed the area shortly after noon and headed for Halifax, where she arrived early on Tuesday, April 30. In her holds and stacked on her decks were the remains of 190 of *Titanic*'s victims.

The Cable Ship Minia *was the second vessel chartered by the White Star Line for the recovery operation.*

CHAPTER 7

RECOVERY CONTINUES

MINIA

ALTHOUGH *MACKAY-BENNETT* IS CERTAINLY the most well known of the ships that recovered the bodies of *Titanic* victims, she was not the only one. In the end, the White Star Line chartered three other vessels to complete the task, while four other passing ships also picked up bodies from the North Atlantic. By the time it became obvious that additional vessels would be required to recover all the bodies that were being reported by ships passing through *Titanic*'s floating wreckage, the White Star Line had already arranged for a second ship to sail. The Cable Ship *Minia* was owned by Western Union and was under the command of Captain William deCarteret.

Captain William deCarteret was in command of Minia.

Minia left Halifax on Monday, April 22, carrying undertaker William Snow, the Reverend Henry Ward Cunningham of Saint George's Anglican Church, 150 coffins, 20 tons of ice, and 15 tons of scrap iron. The ship's surgeon, Dr. William Mosher, assisted Snow in his undertaking duties. *Minia*'s crew took over their solemn task from *Mackay-Bennett* on Friday, April 26. Second Electrician Francis Dyke of *Minia* called it "the most remarkable trip the old *Minia* has ever been on" and described the grim experience in a letter to his mother: "I can tell you none of us like this job at all but it is better to recover them properly than to let them float around for weeks...I expected to see the poor creatures disfigured but they all look as calm as if they were asleep." Snow called the process "bodysnatching."

Minia found few victims because bodies and wreckage were being scattered east and north by the Gulf Stream, some as far as 150 miles from the spot where *Titanic* went down. Dyke noted that once bodies were in the Gulf Stream "they go very fast" and speculated that "many will be washed up on the Irish Coast." By this point in the recovery, the crew seldom found two or more bodies together. While there were fewer bodies, there was plenty of debris, and crewmen picked up several pieces of wood and other objects from *Titanic*. In a letter to his sister, Snow listed some of these as "deck chairs, doors, chests of drawers, two of the steps of the grand stairway, some beautiful carved panels (oak) and cords of painted wood, moulding, boards" and noted that "everyone is making checkerboards, cribbage boards or paper weights" from *Titanic* wreckwood. Snow himself "found a card signed by Ismay in the pocket of one of the stewards" whose body was recovered and which he was keeping as his "chief souvenir."

During her time on station, *Minia* recovered only seventeen bodies, all men. On the first day, the crew found eleven bodies (Nos. 307–317), then one per day

TOP *A boat crew from* Minia *recover a body. In all, her sailors found seventeen bodies.*
BOTTOM *The recovered body of a male victim is embalmed aboard* Minia. *His face is discreetly hidden behind a bottle of embalming fluid to conceal his identity.*

for the next four days (Nos. 318–321), and finally two bodies on May 1 (Nos. 322–323). No bodies were recovered on May 2, so *Minia* departed the area on Friday, May 3. Of the recovered remains, only two unidentified bodies were buried at sea, both believed to be firemen. Speculation is that these bodies must have been badly disfigured or decomposed, as *Minia* certainly had sufficient supplies on board to embalm several bodies.

Although clergymen were aboard the recovery ships to perform burials at sea, they were also there to provide moral and spiritual support for their crews. Recovering the bloated, stiff, and disfigured bodies of men, women, and—especially—little children was not the regular job of these cable-laying sailors, and the experience would have been extremely difficult for even the most hardened among them. In appreciation of the support that Reverend Cunningham provided to them, *Minia*'s crew presented him with a *Titanic* deck chair recovered from the wreckage. Cunningham's grandson later donated it to Halifax's Maritime Museum of the Atlantic, where today it is a principal artifact in the museum's outstanding *Titanic* exhibition.

This photograph of a parade in the naval dockyard in 1902 shows many of the sites later associated with Titanic *victims. The high stone wall surrounding the dockyard kept spectators out, while hearses carrying recovered bodies travelled up the North Street hill towards the temporary morgue on Agricola Street. Families and friends arrived at the Intercolonial Railway station on the right, and any bodies sent home for burial were shipped from the station.*

The bodies of the other fifteen victims were taken to Halifax for disposition. They included a first-class passenger, a second-class passenger, three third-class passengers, and ten crew members, all but one identified. The most prominent of these victims was Charles Hays, president of the Grand Trunk Railway. *Minia* arrived at Halifax in the early morning hours of Monday, May 6, and waited at the quarantine inspection station at the mouth of the harbour until dawn. She then proceeded up the harbour as *Mackay-Bennett* had to Coaling Jetty 4 in the naval dockyard to unload her cargo. *Minia*'s unused coffins and other supplies were turned over to the Canadian government vessel *Montmagny*, the next ship to search the North Atlantic for bodies.

MONTMAGNY

ALTHOUGH IT WAS becoming obvious that there were very few bodies left to recover from *Titanic*, the White Star Line chartered the Canadian Government Ship *Montmagny* to continue the search. *Montmagny* was a lighthouse supply and buoy tender operated by the Department of Marine and Fisheries. She left Sorel, Quebec, for Halifax under command of her regular captain, François-Xavier Pouliot. In Halifax, the ship picked up supplies, plus two undertakers,

The Canadian Government Ship Montmagny *was the third chartered vessel to search for* Titanic's *victims. She recovered only four bodies.*

John Snow, Jr. (who had been on *Mackay-Bennett*), and Cecil Zink of Dartmouth Undertakers, as well as two clergymen, the Reverend Samuel Prince of St. Paul's Anglican Church and Father Patrick McQuillan from St. Mary's Roman Catholic Basilica. Unusually, she also picked up a second captain, Peter Johnson, an experienced East Coast skipper. In the international waters where the search for bodies was conducted, Johnson was technically in command, although in all likelihood the two captains cooperated fully in their task.

Montmagny made two trips to the area where *Titanic* sank. On her first trip, she departed Halifax on May 6. Despite poor weather, the crew found a single body (No. 326—for some reason Nos. 324–325 were not used) on Thursday, May 9, an unidentified male who was possibly a steward. His remains were buried at sea. After three more victims (Nos. 327–329) were found the next day, *Montmagny* departed the search area and docked at Louisbourg on Cape Breton Island on Monday, May 13. The three bodies were shipped to Halifax by train.

After taking on more supplies, *Montmagny* returned to the search area the next day and sailed eastwards as far as the Gulf Stream. Although a few pieces of scattered wood were spotted, *Montmagny* did not find any more bodies. She continued her search until May 19, when the ship received a relayed wireless message to abandon the search and return to Halifax. Before *Montmagny* departed she met the last of chartered search vessels, *Algerine*, at about 6:00 P.M. On May 23, *Montmagny* arrived in Halifax and recommenced her regular duties for the Department of Marine and Fisheries.

ALGERINE AND *FLORIZEL*

ALGERINE WAS A CIVILIAN cargo and passenger ship, as well as a part-time sealer, owned by Bowring Brothers of St. John's, Newfoundland. She was the fourth and last vessel chartered by the White Star Line to search for the bodies of *Titanic* victims. *Algerine* sailed on May 16 under the command of Captain John Jackman with two St. John's undertakers aboard, Andrew Carnell and a Mr. Lawrence. It is not known if a clergyman sailed with them. After a rendezvous with *Montmagny*, *Algerine* searched for three weeks but found only a single body (No. 330), the last one recovered by a contracted ship. The remains of saloon steward James McGrady were taken to St. John's, where they were transferred to another vessel, *Florizel*, on June 6. *Florizel* was a passenger liner and the flagship of the Bowring Brothers Red Cross Line. Two days later, *Florizel* sailed for Halifax, arriving on June 11.

The passenger liner Florizel *was the flagship of Bowring Brothers Red Cross Line of Newfoundland. She carried the remains of James McGrady to Halifax, the last body to be recovered by a contracted ship.*

CARPATHIA

WHEN *CARPATHIA* ARRIVED on the scene of the *Titanic* sinking at four o'clock on the morning of April 15, besides picking up survivors, her crew also recovered four bodies. Additionally, three other ships besides those chartered by the White Star Line found the bodies of five *Titanic* victims. None of these nine bodies were assigned numbers and all were buried at sea. Very few references for the *Titanic* tragedy make any mention of these last few recovered victims.

During the U.S. Senate inquiry, *Carpathia's* captain, Arthur Rostron, stated that during the rescue operation, his crew took three dead men who had died of exposure out of *Titanic's* lifeboats. He also noted that another man was brought up, whom he thought was probably one of the crew, and who died at about ten o'clock that morning. All four were buried that afternoon at four o'clock. Although Rostron did not know their names, he said one of his officers and *Titanic's* officers had identified them from their belongings.

The dead were identified as first-class passenger William Hoyt (who had jumped into the water to reach the lifeboat carrying his wife), third-class passenger David Livshin of Manchester, England—who was travelling to Montreal under the name of Abraham Harmer—and two crewmen, bedroom steward Sidney Siebert and able seaman William Lyons. Hoyt was a big man and the survivors in Lifeboat 14 had difficulty hauling him out of the water. When he was pulled in he was bleeding from the nose and mouth. At the inquiry Fifth Officer Lowe stated, "...we took off his collar so as to give him more chance to breathe, but unfortunately, he died. He was too far gone when we picked him up."

Captain Arthur Rostron of Carpathia *became a hero for rescuing* Titanic's *survivors.*

There are several questions surrounding Livshin. He may have been picked up by Lifeboat 14 or he may have been transferred from overturned Collapsible B to Lifeboat 12. He was certainly dead by the time *Carpathia* arrived on the scene and his body was taken aboard her. His wife did not know any reason why he would be travelling under the name Harmer. The best guess is that perhaps he had purchased the ticket from a third party. In the case of the two crew members, Siebert and Lyons swam to and were picked up by Lifeboat 4. Siebert soon died in the boat, but Lyons lived a little longer. He lost consciousness and was transferred to *Carpathia*, where he later died.

Over the years, various numbers and identities have been given for *Titanic* victims buried from *Carpathia*. The numbers range from three to as many as ten. Some accounts have one of the bodies as that of Marconi wireless operator Jack Phillips, but these have largely been discounted because of the distinct uniform that Phillips wore, which would have been clearly recognized. Another account states Lyons was dead when he was brought aboard *Carpathia* and that it was Siebert who died later. As with so many of the questions surrounding *Titanic*, the answer to this discrepancy may never be found.

OCEANIC

UNTIL 1901, White Star's *Oceanic* was the largest ship in the world and the first to exceed the length of Brunel's *Great Eastern*. Constructed as the line's flagship, during the coal strike *Oceanic* was temporarily laid up in Southampton so that White Star's latest showpiece, *Titanic*, would have enough coal for her maiden voyage. When *Titanic* sailed on April 10, her massive displacement pulled *Oceanic* so far away from her berth that an eighteen-metre gangway fell into the water in the same incident that pulled the American liner *New York* away from her berth.

Titanic's Second Officer Charles Lightoller, usually regarded as one of the heroes of the disaster and the most senior officer to survive the sinking, had served on *Oceanic* on two occasions before he went to *Titanic*. In his autobiography, *Titanic and Other Ships*, he noted, "I got my severest mail boat training during seven hard, though happy years I spent in the Queen of Seas, as the *Oceanic* was then called. A wonderful ship, built in a class of her own, and by herself." Another forty-eight *Titanic* crew members had also served in her.

At noon on May 13, almost a full month after the sinking, *Oceanic* discovered *Titanic's* Collapsible A, some 322 kilometres southeast of the sinking. It contained three badly decomposed bodies: first-class passenger Thomson Beattie of Winnipeg, as well as a steward and a fireman, both unidentified. Later research has suggested one of these might have been Arthur Keefe, a third-class passenger from New Jersey. After drifting in Lifeboat 4 for some time after *Titanic* went down, Fifth Officer Harold Lowe spotted Collapsible A and rowed to it. He hauled its dozen still-living occupants (and one corpse) into his lifeboat, leaving three bodies behind, those of victims who had apparently died of exposure shortly after the sinking. He then removed the sea plugs while someone put lifebelts over their faces and set the collapsible adrift. According to his testimony before the U.S. Senate committee, when he asked the survivors if they were sure the remaining three were dead, he received the reply, "Absolutely sure."

A passenger aboard *Oceanic*, Sir Shane Leslie, described the discovery of an "open lifeboat floating in mid Atlantic":

> *What was horrifying was that it contained three prostrate figures. Orders from the bridge dispatched a lifeboat with an officer and a medical officer. What followed was ghastly. Two sailors could be seen, their hair bleached by exposure to sun and salt, and a third figure wearing full evening dress flat on the benches. All three were dead... The boat was full of ghastly souvenirs, such as rings and watches and even children's shoes from those who had been unrescued and had been consigned to the ocean one by one.*

Due to the advanced state of decomposition, all three bodies were quickly buried at sea. In a letter published in the *Times* (London) on May 30, another passenger, Harry Crunch, noted, "we could plainly see the three men in it. It was the most pathetic sight I have ever witnessed." According to Crunch, "As quickly as possible a boat was lowered. They rowed out, and then after a few minutes came back to report. They then took tarpaulins and big iron weights, and the doctor also went out and read the burial service over them and they were buried in the sea." Beattie's body was buried on his mother's birthday, ironically at almost the same spot in the Atlantic where she had been born eighty-two years earlier on a ship headed for Canada.

FROZEN OR STARVED?

There was no water or food on the boat, but the doctor told Crunch he saw "small bits of cork which had been chewed." Other newspaper reports published on May 17, the same day that *Oceanic* docked in New York, carried similar stories. The *Orange County Times-Press* noted that "each victim had pieces of cork in his mouth indicating that they had tried to keep themselves from starving," while the *St. Paul Daily News* stated, "Bits of cork in their mouths and tooth marks on the cork and wood portions of the boat indicated" death by starvation.

Dead men do not eat cork—or anything else for that matter. Could it be that after surviving *Titanic's* sinking and making it into the collapsible, the three men were unconscious and, in the darkness and hurry of the others to get into Lifeboat 14, suffered the cruel fate of being abandoned and subsequently starved to death? If so, it is hard to imagine the despair the three men must have felt as they drifted aimlessly in the vast ocean, desperately waiting for a ship to appear on the horizon, growing weaker by the hour. As Collapsible A was found on a major shipping lane, some ships may even have been spotted by its occupants, but the tiny speck remained unseen to passing crews and passengers. White Star Line officials were quick to discredit the theory that the three had starved, pointing out Lowe's testimony before the Senate committee. "The sea was full of floating cork," their statement read, "and finding of these particles does not lend credence to the starvation theory." Or does it?

THE THREE BODIES in Collapsible A were not the last *Titanic* victims to be found; two more were discovered in June. SS *Ottawa*, an Anglo-American Oil Company tanker, sailed under command of Captain R. G. Tait. A letter written on June 6 by Third Officer Thomas Cook on the back of a United States government form for reporting the weather and held in Washington's national archives describes an amazing incident:

> [W]e *picked up the body of a man wearing a lifebelt. We put our boat out and searched his clothes and found a wallet bearing the initials W. T. K. and evidently a passenger of the Titanic. It contained a love letter and a business card, "Apartments" in Margate, Kent. The man was buried with ceremony of the Church of England. The body was much decomposed, especially the hands and face. There was no name on the lifebelt as it has been washed off. We have since ascertained that his name is W. T. Kerley and was an assistant steward on the* Titanic. *The finding of the body was 543 miles from* Titanic's *position."*

Kerley seems neither to have been counted among the identified dead nor as one of the bodies of those recovered. He was found well after the American and British inquiries were completed and almost two months after the disaster, at a time when the *Titanic* story was old news. Kerley was a single assistant saloon steward; *Titanic* was his first ship.

Two days after *Ottawa*'s gruesome discovery and fifty-four days after the *Titanic* went down, a British steamship, SS *Ilford*, found the last certified victim of the disaster. William Cheverton was a saloon steward who had been with *Titanic* since she first sailed from Belfast. He had previously worked in *Olympic*. In all, 337 bodies of passengers and crew were recovered by various ships after the sinking, 128 of which joined the other victims in the deep.

Saloon steward William Cheverton was the last of Titanic's *victims to be found.*

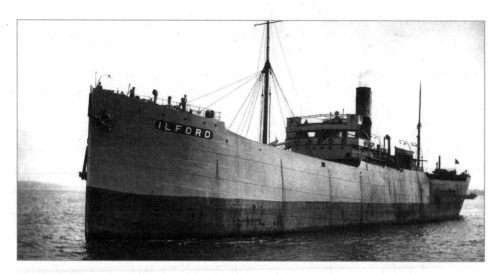

The ss Ilford *found the body of steward William Cheverton, the last victim recovered from the* Titanic *disaster.*

Bodies Recovered at Sea

Vessel	No. of Bodies Recovered	Dates Bodies Recovered	Disposition
RMS *Carpathia*	4 (unnumbered)	April 15	buried at sea
CS *Mackay-Bennett*	306 (Nos. 1-306)	April 21-26	116 buried at sea, 190 taken to Halifax
CS *Minia*	17 (Nos. 307-323)	April 26-May 3	2 buried at sea, 15 taken to Halifax
CGS *Montmagny*	4 (Nos. 326-329*)	May 9-10	1 buried at sea, 3 sent to Halifax
RMS *Oceanic*	3 (unnumbered)	May 13	buried at sea
SS *Algerine*	1 (No. 330)	May 22	sent to Halifax
SS *Ottawa*	1 (unnumbered)	June 6	buried at sea
SS *Ilford*	1 (unnumbered)	June 8	buried at sea
Total	337		Total 128 buried at sea, 209 taken to Halifax, 150 buried in Halifax

Nos. 324-325 were not used

Mackay-Bennett *steams into Halifax Harbour.*

CHAPTER 8

HOME PORTS

ARRIVAL IN HALIFAX

AFTER TWO GRISLY WEEKS AT SEA, *Mackay-Bennett*—the media's "Death Ship"—slowly steamed into Halifax harbour at nine o'clock on the pale grey morning of Tuesday, April 30. On board were 190 of the 306 bodies her crew had recovered from the ocean. From the shore, spectators saw "her afterdeck piled high with coffins and on her forward a hundred unshrouded bodies," according to the *Halifax Herald.* Unseen—and unreported—were several other bodies crammed into the forward hold, piled on top of each other under a tarpaulin.

Although the authorities had made arrangements to accept her tragic cargo, Haligonians also showed their empathy for the families of the victims. Many windows of local businesses were draped in black and some of them displayed framed

Access to Halifax's naval dockyard was controlled through its guarded main gate.

photographs of *Titanic*. In reality, the photo showed her sister ship, *Olympic*, as no pictures of *Titanic* were available. As *Mackay-Bennett* made her way up the harbour, church and fire bells tolled and flags flew at half-mast. Solemn spectators stood on Citadel Hill, lined the waterfront, and packed the rooftops of houses and other buildings to get a better view. Additional coffins were stacked high at the dockside and the new Mayflower Curling Club nearby on Agricola Street had been turned into a temporary morgue. Across the street from the dockyard was the Intercolonial Railway Station, where reporters and relatives had arrived in Halifax, and from where any bodies sent home would be shipped.

At 9:30, *Mackay-Bennett* docked at the naval yard, just as the sun came out from behind the clouds. The crowds stood silent and the men removed their hats. The dockyard had been chosen because it was behind a high stone wall and out of sight of the curious and gathered reporters. Horse-drawn hearses, as well as a few other wagons pressed into service, waited on the dock. All had been checked by some of the twenty sailors and four petty officers from HMCS *Niobe*, as well as several men from the Dominion Police, as they entered the naval yard to ensure that no unauthorized individuals tried to sneak in from the crowd assembled around the dockyard gates. Mourners and officials who carried passes signed by Commander Martin, the dockyard commandant, were also allowed to enter, most of the former in a variety of closed vehicles to ensure their privacy.

But one resourceful local reporter had managed to scoop his colleagues. Before *Mackay-Bennett* sailed on her grim task, Jim Hickey, the *Halifax Chronicle*'s news editor, had made arrangements with Canon Hind to obtain exclusive details about the dead. As *Mackay-Bennett* sailed up the harbour, Hickey approached her in a hired tugboat. Once he was alongside, Hind threw him a bottle containing a list of the identified dead. Their names appeared in the newspaper before the coroner's office even had them.

It took three and a half hours to unload the 190 bodies from the ship. The shrouded and unshrouded bodies were taken off on stretchers, each stretcher carried by two sailors, bare-headed as a mark of respect for the dead. On the dock, each body was placed in a waiting coffin and then loaded onto a hearse. The bodies that had been placed in coffins at sea were last, each one swung over

Coaling Wharf 4 in the naval dockyard, where Mackay-Bennett *tied up to keep spectators away.*

Hearses wait dockside to transport Titanic's *victims to the Mayflower Curling Club.*

the side and lowered to the dock. As soon as a hearse was filled, it left the dock-yard, its cargo saluted by the naval sentries who manned the gates. While most of the thirty hearses and wagons went directly to the Mayflower Curling Club, apparently ten of them—undoubtedly carrying the remains of first-class passengers—went instead to Snow's funeral home.

Halfway through the unloading process, at 11:15, Captain Larnder held a news briefing aboard his ship for fifteen reporters from a variety of Canadian and American newspapers. Canon Hind and John Snow, Jr., also spoke, with the minister commending the crew of *Mackay-Bennett* for the way in which they had acquitted themselves during their arduous task. The undertaker was quoted in the *Evening Mail*: "There was awful evidence of the fierce struggle for life, hands clutching wildly at clothing, faces distorted with terror." Snow later denied he had ever made this statement.

Many of the bodies that arrived in Halifax were still unidentified and the immediate problem became how to handle so many remains. John Henry Barnstead, the deputy registrar of deaths for Nova Scotia, developed a system

Unidentified bodies arrive at the Mayflower Curling Club (building on left) for embalming.

to list all personal effects and descriptions of the bodies, whether they seemed significant or not. Barnstead's system was used five years later to identify the victims of the horrendous 1917 Halifax Explosion. Several bodies were difficult to identify because there was nothing on them to indicate who they were. Many people had left the ship in a hurry, some wearing only a jacket or a coat over their nightwear, and did not have any papers on them. Many crewmen were recognized from some form of uniform they were wearing, but several others had been asleep and were not in uniform.

The White Star Line had made arrangements to receive the bodies in Halifax and contracted Snow's funeral business to handle all the remains. Five hundred coffins and caskets were ordered from Ontario, while Snow gathered forty embalmers from across Nova Scotia and elsewhere in the Maritimes. Two female embalmers came from Saint John, New Brunswick. Sisters Annie O'Neill and Elizabeth Walsh embalmed the women and the only child brought to Halifax. The line also arranged large burial plots in the non-denominational Fairview Lawn Cemetery, as well as the Roman Catholic Mount Olivet Cemetery. As the largest

The ice floor of the Mayflower Curling Club was divided into enclosed cubicles for relatives to view and identify remains.

refrigerated building in Halifax, the Mayflower Curling Club was chosen as a temporary morgue. It was also relatively close to the dockyard and had a large glassed-in viewing area. Before relatives could claim bodies, identification had to be confirmed, a death certificate and burial permit issued, and embalming completed. Despite the fact that most victims had succumbed to hypothermia, cause of death was invariably listed as "drowning."

Perhaps the thorniest issue was the best method for identification of remains by relatives, especially since disfigurement due to injury or time in the water had rendered some victims impossible to identify. On April 29, at a meeting of the "mourners"—as the press had dubbed family and friends who travelled to Halifax—procedures were decided. Preparation would take place out of sight in an area behind a newly constructed wooden partition, where thirty-four embalmers' benches were installed. Once a body was embalmed, it would be brought out to one of sixty-seven enclosed cubicles, each capable of holding three coffins. Where the name of the deceased was known, relatives could then view the body to confirm identity. The way one relative was identified caused a shock to embalmer Frank Newell of Yarmouth. He unexpectedly discovered the body of his uncle, Bostonian Arthur Newell, among the remains and collapsed.

Families were given the option of having the remains of their relatives shipped home, and several took advantage of this offer. In the end, of the 209 bodies recovered to Halifax, 59 were shipped to other parts of Canada (7), the United States (39), Britain (8), and even further afield (5: 1 each to Uruguay, Belgium, Italy, Denmark, and Norway) for burial. They included 31 first-class passengers, 14 second-class passengers, 11 third-class passengers, 1 crew member, and 2 other individuals who, although they worked on the ship (a bandsman and a postal supervisor), were not considered part of the crew.

FAMILIES

THE REMAINS OF two sets of relatives were sent from Halifax, a father and son and a married couple. One of these was the first body recovered, a young boy with light hair. For warmth against the cold night air—and possibly an even colder ocean—he wore a grey overcoat on top of two other coats, as well as a woollen sweater and a shirt. His personal effects consisted of a purse containing a few Danish coins and a ring, plus two handkerchiefs marked with an "A." The body was later identified at Halifax from his effects as that of nine-year-old third-class passenger Walter van Billiard, who had embarked at Southampton with his father, Austin, and ten-year-old brother, James.

Although James's remains were never found, his father's body was the 255th recovered. Austin van Billiard was originally from North Wales, Pennsylvania, but had travelled to France to find work as an electrician at Paris's 1900 Universal Exposition. There, he met and married Maud Murray, an English girl. James and Walter were born within two and a half years of the marriage and in 1906 the family moved to South Africa to try their luck at diamond mining. After six years

The relatives of Titanic's *victims arrived and departed Halifax at the Intercolonial Railway Station. Any remains sent elsewhere for burial were also shipped from the station.*

of harsh conditions (and two more children), Austin decided to return to the United States and try his hand as a diamond merchant. The Van Billiards first travelled to London, where Maud's parents lived, so she could recover her health after their years in Africa. Austin took his two eldest children aboard *Titanic*, leaving Maud and the rest of the family to join them later.

Austin's body was identified from his personal effects, including twelve uncut diamonds. At his parents' request, Austin's body was shipped on May 4 to North Wales, Pennsylvania. Despite the doubtful evidence about Walter's identification, Body No. 1 was shipped as well. Father and son were buried on May 8. The next year Maud and the two surviving children moved to North Wales to join her parents-in-law, whom neither she nor her children had met. Over the years, there has been some doubt expressed as to the reliability of the identification of Walter, especially given the presence of Danish coins. This has led some researchers to believe the body could have been another child. Only the handkerchiefs bearing the letter "A"—possibly his father's—seem to be the questionable basis for this identification.

The married couple also sent from Halifax were Mr. and Mrs. Alexander Robins. Grace Charity Robins's body was the seventh one recovered. She was a third-class passenger whose identification was based on a purse inscribed "A. Robins," as well as documents. Charity and her husband, Alexander, a stonemason, were returning to their home in Yonkers, New York, accompanied by her nephew, William Nancarrow. They had been visiting relatives in Cornwall, from where they had earlier emigrated to the United States. Alexander's body was the 119th recovered and was identified from personal belongings. The possessions found on his remains are another example of the often extensive items carried by many of the victims.

Alexander's effects included a gold watch with chain and seal; another gold watch with chain and locket; a silver watch; the interior works of a Waltham watch (a high-quality watch produced in Waltham, Massachusetts, which, incidentally, was used by the Canadian Pacific Railway); three knives; two pipes; a cigarette holder; a cigar holder; keys; a gold ring; a hair comb; two pocket diaries and papers. In addition, Alexander was carrying a surprisingly large sum of money for someone travelling third class: IMM cheques totalling $2,500; £41 in gold, plus 37 shillings and 6 pence in a purse. The Robinses' remains were sent to their daughter in Yonkers and buried there.

In many cases only one family member's body was recovered. Body No. 142 was identified from a third-class ticket found on it as Carl Asplund, a Swedish labourer. He also had six other tickets, those of his wife and their five children, ranging in age from three to thirteen, including a set of twins. The entire family made it to the boat deck, where Selma, a three-year-old son, and a five-year-old daughter were put into Lifeboat 15. Carl and three boys, aged five, nine, and thirteen, remained behind and died. Only Carl's body was found. On Selma's instructions, it was shipped to Worcester, Massachusetts, on May 3, where Carl was buried in the Swedish Cemetery. Similarly, only Ernest Danbom's body (No. 197) was recovered, while those of his wife and baby son were not, nor were any of the seven Andersson family members who were travelling with them. Like Carl Asplund's remains, Ernest's body was shipped to the United States, to Stanton, Iowa.

CHEATING HUSBANDS

THE FIRST OF THE first-class remains recovered was Body No. 16, identified from his pocketbook as George Rosenshine of New York. There was a bit of skulduggery involved in his story. Rosenshine was a forty-six-year-old import merchant travelling under the assumed name of George Thorne with his thirty-eight-year-old mistress, Gertrude Maybelle Thorne. The two had embarked at Cherbourg after a combined business trip and holiday. Gertrude was saved in Collapsible D. George's body was claimed by his brother and shipped to New York, where he was buried in a family plot in the Bayside Cemetery, Brooklyn.

American cinematographer William H. Harbeck (Body No. 35) was a forty-four-year-old second-class passenger, who was married and had two teenage sons. One of the first moving picture filmmakers, he established his reputation by filming the destruction caused by the 1906 San Francisco Earthquake, which led the Canadian Pacific Railway to hire him to make promotional films for them. Harbeck produced thirteen one-reelers for the CPR designed to attract European emigrants to the Canadian west. They were so successful the company renewed his contract and sent him to Paris in the spring of 1912 to study with a French filmmaker who was a master of the outdoor location shot. While in Europe, he also filmed sights in several countries for eventual showing in American theatres.

Harbeck seems to have been up to the same type of marital deception as George Rosenshine. The woman he was travelling with, whom other passengers assumed was his young wife, was actually Henriette Yrois, a twenty-four-year-old French model he had met in Paris. They were on their way to Montreal, where he was due to make additional films for the CPR. When Harbeck's body was found, it was clutching Henriette's purse, which contained his wedding ring.

If second-class passenger Stanley Fox (Body No. 236) was not involved in the same sort of deception as George Rosenshine and William Harbeck, it certainly appears that other members of his family were. It began innocently enough with instructions to ship his body to his widow in Rochester, New York, on "Order of Mrs. Emma Fox." Except Fox's wife's name was Cora, not Emma, and the usual terminology for shipping remains contained the term "instructions from." Perhaps this was nothing more than clerical errors, but then events became decidedly murky.

A woman who called herself Lydia Fox arrived in Halifax, accompanied by an unidentified man. She claimed to be the sister-in-law of Stanley's widow, who was too upset to travel, so she would be taking the body to Rochester. Lydia was married to Stanley's older brother, but it is not believed that he was her escort for this trip. Her credentials confirmed, the authorities released Fox's body to her, which was loaded on a train. Just before the train departed however, two telegrams arrived from Cora Fox. The first one, to the authorities, asked them not to give the body to Lydia and retain Stanley's belongings, while the second one, to the undertaker, stated Lydia had no right to claim the body. Lydia told the undertaker she had no idea why such a telegram had been sent to him, while the authorities, a bit perplexed, pondered their next move. By this stage, Lydia, her companion, and Fox's body—but not his personal effects—were already on the train and leaving Halifax.

Belatedly, the authorities telegraphed the station in Truro, one hundred kilometres away, to remove the coffin from the train and keep it there. Lydia was unaware of this and continued on her trip to Rochester without the body. Later, the mayor of Rochester contacted Halifax officials on Cora's behalf and the body and effects were finally shipped to her for burial. Insurance fraud, publicity, and family disapproval of Stanley's choice of a wife—perhaps due to concerns over her social standing—have all been suggested as the reason behind this incident, but nothing is known for certain. It certainly was not for Stanley's personal effects: all that was found with the body was the equivalent of about $70 in American and British currency and two watches.

MILLIONAIRES

SEVERAL OF THE millionaires aboard *Titanic* were lost in the disaster. The richest was John Jacob Astor IV, who saw his wife into a lifeboat but was not

*Isidor and Ida Straus decided to go down with
Titanic rather than be separated.*

allowed to enter it himself. Astor's body (No. 124) was reportedly soot-covered and crushed beyond recognition, likely the result of the forward funnel falling over on him. He was identified by the initials "J. J. A." on the back of his shirt collar. Astor's nineteen-year-old son, Vincent, travelled to Halifax to claim his father's body and took it back to New York City on May 1 in a private railcar. Astor was buried in the family mausoleum. Madeleine Astor went on to two more marriages, both of which ended in divorce. When she died of a heart attack in 1940, she bequeathed the pearl necklace she had worn in the lifeboat, valued at the time at $1,525, to another son, John Jacob Astor VI. Later, it was purchased by Dorothy, the wife of Nova Scotian millionaire financier Izaak Walton Killam.

Although the remains of Isidor Straus (Body No. 96) were recovered, those of his devoted wife who opted to stay with him to the end were never found. His body was delivered to Maurice Rothschild in Halifax and taken to New York, where he was interred in a private mausoleum in the Bronx's Woodlawn Cemetery. Forty thousand people attended the couple's memorial service, where one of the eulogies was given by Andrew Carnegie. In 1914, Bloomingdale Square in New York City, a block from where they lived, was renamed Straus Park in their honour. On a memorial in the park a passage from 2 Samuel 23 refers to Ida's decision to stay with Isidor: "Lovely and pleasant were they in their lives and in their death they were not parted." Isidor's servant, John Farthing, also died in the sinking; Ida's maid, Ellen Bird, survived.

Hud Allison's body (No. 135) was the first to be taken from the *Mackay-Bennett* directly to the Intercolonial Railway Station for shipment to his brother Percy in Montreal. Percy took the body to Chesterville, Ontario, the site of their stock farm, and buried him the next day in the Maple Grove Cemetery in nearby Winchester. Two months later, the two dozen horses Hud had purchased in Scotland and that sailed on a different ship were delivered to Percy at the Winchester train station. Today, a large obelisk marks the Allison family burials in the Maple Grove Cemetery.

The remains of Charles Hays (Body No. 307), president of the Grand Trunk Railway, were the first to be recovered by *Minia* after she arrived in the disaster area. According to electrician Francis Dyke, "It was no trouble to identify him as he had a lot of papers on him and a watch with his name on." Initially Hays was reported in several newspapers as being a survivor. In Halifax, his body was delivered to Grand Trunk's vice-president and taken in Hays's private railcar "Canada" for burial in Montreal's Mount Royal Cemetery. Grand Trunk Railway officials felt Hays's body might not be found, so they had earlier ordered a memorial tribute held in the company's offices around the world. At 11:30 A.M. Montreal time on April 25, a five-minute period of silence was observed in Grand Trunk offices in Canada, the United States, and Britain, as well as by staff of affiliated railroads, hotels, and steamship lines. His body was recovered the next day. The gloves Hays was wearing when his body was found are on display in the Maritime Museum of the Atlantic in Halifax.

OTHER CANADIANS

BESIDES HUD ALLISON and Charles Hays, the remains of other Canadians or those travelling to Canada were also recovered. Of the three British Hickman brothers on their way to Manitoba, Lewis's (No. 256) was the only one recovered. Initially, the body was identified as that of his brother, Leonard, because Lewis had grabbed his brother's green overcoat before he went out on deck, and it had Leonard's International Order of Foresters membership card in a pocket. When

Leonard's colleagues in Manitoba learned that he was to be buried in Halifax, they paid to have the body shipped to Neepawa and fellow lodge member Harold Honeyman had a tombstone engraved with his name. The body arrived an hour before the funeral and when the coffin was

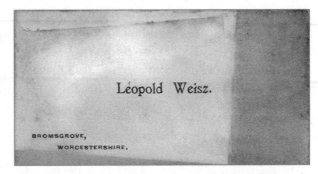

The body of Léopold Weisz was identified by this calling card.

opened Honeyman was shocked to find it was not Leonard. With the church packed and the funeral about to commence, Honeyman closed the casket and the funeral took place. Only after Hickman's effects were returned to his family in England did Lewis's wife begin to suspect it was not Leonard that was buried, but her husband. When asked, Honeyman confirmed her suspicions. Later, the inscription on the tombstone was changed to list all three brothers who died.

In keeping with the T. Eaton Company's policy of looking after its employees, all arrangements for buyer George Graham (Body No. 147) were made by the firm. His remains were sent to Toronto on April 30, accompanied by an undertaker. Graham's funeral was held in Harriston, Ontario, his wife Edith's hometown, and attended by fifty store employees brought from Toronto on a special train, which also carried Graham's casket. Memorial services were also held in Winnipeg and Toronto, the location of the company's two stores, and both stores closed for a half day on April 20. The night *Titanic* went down, Graham had dined with four other travelling salesmen, who autographed a menu as a souvenir of the voyage. Of the five, only Graham perished. In 1911, his three-year-old son had been buried in his hometown of St. Mary's. When Edith died in 1960, she was buried beside her son in accordance with her wishes. Graham's family then had his body exhumed from Harriston and reinterred beside his wife and son.

The body of Thomas Beattie's friend, banker Thomas McCaffry (No. 292), was recovered in less dramatic circumstances than Beattie's (Beattie was one of three bodies found in Collapsible A). It was sent to Montreal for burial, where he had been raised. Their mutual friend and travelling companion, Hugo Ross, had remained ill in his cabin since departing Southampton. Sometime after the collision, Arthur Peuchen encountered Ross on the grand staircase, still in his pyjamas. When Peuchen told him they had struck an iceberg, Ross replied that he was sick and that it would take "more than an iceberg to get me off this ship." Ross returned to his room; his body was never found.

Stone carver Léopold Weisz (Body No. 293) was identified by his calling card as well as "W. L." marked on his shirt. He carried a small fortune: when authorities examined his clothes they found $30,000 in currency (some sources state in addition to $15,000 in gold) sewn into the lining of his suit. His wife, Mathilde, survived in Lifeboat 10. Aboard *Carpathia* she alternated between being a grieving widow and a tower of strength for some of the other survivors, and was especially kind in helping Juliette Laroche and Antoinine Mallet with their young children. Until Léopold's body was found, Mathilde was in danger of being deported to England as an indigent. Léopold's remains were forwarded to Montreal for burial on April 30 in that city's Baron de Hirsch Cemetery.

"FOREIGNERS"

THE BODIES OF five individuals were shipped further afield than North America or Britain. One of these was sent to South America, while the other four went to continental Europe. The body of Ramon Artagaveytia, a seventy-one-year-old Uruguayan businessman (estimated age sixty—a rare case of the authorities having underestimated) travelling first class, was the twenty-second pulled from the ocean. He was identified by the initials "R. A." on several pieces of underwear and a watch with his name on it. Artagaveytia's family had a long relationship with the sea. In 1871, he was one of only sixty-five passengers to survive the fire and sinking of *America* off the coast of Uruguay, which killed ninety-nine of his fellow passengers and affected him psychologically for the rest of his life. Artagaveytia's remains were delivered to the New York-based Uruguayan Consul in Halifax and forwarded to Uruguay via New York. He was buried in Montevideo on June 18.

The remains shipped to continental Europe for burial were those of first-class passenger Jacob Birnbaum (Body No. 148—Belgium), second-class passengers Sebastiano del Carlo (Body No. 295—Italy) and Jacob Milling (Body No. 271—Denmark), and third-class passenger Sigurd Moen (Body No. 309—Norway).

ARTHUR LAWRENCE WAS a saloon steward whose body was the ninetieth recovered. Lawrence had signed on to deliver *Titanic* from Belfast to Southampton, and then signed on again at Southampton for her transatlantic voyage. Although he gave a Southampton address, his wife, Lily, lived in Rochford, Essex, with their young son, where she ran a small sweet shop. On his widow's instructions his "American casket," which was enclosed in a polished oak coffin with brass fittings, was shipped via Boston to Liverpool, England. On May 13, Lawrence was buried in the West Derby Cemetery, after a funeral that was termed "unique in the history of Liverpool." He was the only crew member sent home for burial.

Wallace Hartley was the leader of Titanic's small band. He bravely inspired his musicians to play until the end.

John March was in a strange position aboard *Titanic*; like the musicians he was neither crew nor passenger. He was one of five postal clerks—three American and two British—who were employees of the U.S. Postal Service and the Royal Mail. Their job was to supervise the carrying of mails under the conditions laid down in the contract awarded to the White Star Line, as well as accept any mail from the passengers or crew. March, an American, was in charge of the small detachment. As rising seawater approached the mail storage area, March, his postal team and a few crewmen struggled to move two hundred bags of registered mail (out of a total of 3,423 mail sacks) to higher decks, where they assumed it would be picked up by a rescue ship. Several surviving passengers later praised their devotion to duty. All five men were lost in the sinking, along with an estimated seven million pieces of mail. March's body (No. 225) was forwarded for burial on May 3 to undertakers in Newark, New Jersey, where he had lived with the younger of his two daughters after his wife had died during surgery the previous year.

The remains of Wallace Henry Hartley (Body No. 224) were identified from his band uniform and items engraved "W. H. H." They were shipped on May 4 to Liverpool via Boston for burial in Colne, Lancashire, where his parents lived.

As would be expected, the hometown funerals of *Titanic* victims attracted large crowds and perhaps the largest was that of Hartley, which forty thousand people attended on May 18. Although the image of the ship's musicians stoically playing as long as they could is one of the most enduring stories from the *Titanic* tragedy, a debate continues over the last piece played. Many initial reports from survivors stated it was the hymn "Nearer My God to Thee," but others said it was "*Songe d'Automne*," or "Autumn," a popular tune at the time. Much could depend on when someone left the ship, as the lifeboats departed over a period of at least an hour and a half. Today, the weight of evidence is that the last song was "Autumn."

An ecumenical service was held for Titanic's *victims at the Brunswick Street Methodist Church on May 3, 1912.*

CHAPTER 9
HALIFAX CEMETERIES

TITANIC GRAVES

OF THE SEVERAL CITIES ASSOCIATED with *Titanic*—Belfast, Southampton, Cherbourg, Queenston, New York, and Halifax—the latter contains the most visible reminder of the great tragedy: the graves of 150 of her victims, who were unclaimed, unidentified, or requested to be buried there by relatives. Between May 1 and June 12, 1912, these 150 bodies were buried in three cemeteries: 121 in non-denominational Fairview Lawn, 19 in Catholic Mount Olivet, and 10 in

Jewish Baron de Hirsch. Both identified and unidentified bodies were buried, but the numbers have changed over the years as additional victims have been identified through dogged detective and forensic work.

On May 3, the first mass burial took place, for unidentified remains. Most of these were presumed to be third class or crew, as it was highly unlikely that their families would have been able to afford a trip to Halifax to identify them. From the beginning, there was no attempt to separate passengers from crew or bury bodies in numerical order. Generally, there were few individual funerals and coffins were taken directly from the temporary morgue to the cemeteries. In most cases the salt-water-damaged clothing the victims were wearing when recovered had been removed for embalming, and it had often been cut off. Additionally, because many victims had valuables sewn into their clothing, a thorough search required further damage to these items. To prevent scavengers from picking through the discarded clothing at the city dump looking for souvenirs or valuables, authorities ordered it burned under police supervision. On the other hand, the personal effects retrieved from the bodies by the medical examiner's staff were delivered by the chief of police to White Star's Halifax agent in 245 canvas bags.

Stonemason Frederick Bishop of the Halifax Marble Works received a contract from the White Star Line for the gravestones of *Titanic* victims. Once the

Fairview Lawn Cemetery headstones rested on their original concrete bases in the 1920s.

graves were filled in, Bishop poured a continuous concrete base at the head of each row, which went down about a metre or so into the earth and stood fifteen centimetres above the ground, to act as a foundation for the later placement of headstones. Because of the slope of the land at Fairview Lawn Cemetery, the concrete bases are stepped in several places. Polished black granite was used for standard headstones: small black rectangles with sloping tops. On these sloping tops, all headstones bear the inscription "Died April 15, 1912," followed by the body number. Where the name was known, it was placed above this inscription. If an individual's identity was discovered later, the name is inscribed on the front of the stone. Relatives were also able to pay to have a headstone of their choice placed on a grave with the inscription they wanted. Eleven such private grave markers were purchased, all in Fairview Lawn. By the end of 1912, headstones began to be placed on the graves.

The White Star Line covered expenses for burials at all three cemeteries and paid for the upkeep of the graves until 1930, when it established a $7,500 fund with the Royal Trust Company for future care. In the mid-1990s, the remaining funds were transferred to the city and apportioned out to the three cemeteries. In 1998, new foundations were made to reset the gravestones. Other improvements, such as improved signage and whitening the letters on the stones, were also made.

FAIRVIEW LAWN CEMETERY

FAIRVIEW LAWN CEMETERY began in 1893 for non-denominational burials. It operated under a private company until 1944, when the city of Halifax took control due to the parent firm's financial difficulties. The city continues to maintain the *Titanic* graves today. White Star's representative, P. V. G. Mitchell, purchased 3,600 square feet in the cemetery for $846.75 and hired land surveyor F. W. Christie to lay out the burial plots.

Row 1 was laid out as a straight trench line and consists of thirty-seven graves, twenty-three of them containing unidentified burials from May 3. Of the identified bodies, five were passengers (two of whom remained unidentified until 1991) and nine were crew. The first victim buried was William Henry Harrison (Body No. 110), private secretary to Ismay, interred on May 1 after a brief service in All Saints Cathedral. Although Harrison's wife wanted his body shipped home to England, this did not happen, perhaps at Ismay's direction to set an example so that other families would not request return of their loved ones. Ismay paid for

Harrison's large headstone, which does not show the body number but contains the inscription "In The Midst Of Life We Are In Death."

Four victims in this row were initially unidentified. Body No. 3 was the first female pulled from the Atlantic. Her clothing and effects included a chemise marked "J. H." in red and she was wearing a grey cholera belt. This body was identified in 1991, when dedicated researchers from the Titanic International Society positively identified her from her effects as Swedish maid Jenny Lovisa Henriksson. She was travelling third class with her cousin to Michigan; the two were going to begin new lives. Henriksson was the only person aboard the ship with the initials "J. H." and additionally wore a cholera belt because of a fear of getting that disease. Cholera belts were an old-fashioned device made of flannel and impregnated with a foul-smelling liquid to prevent their wearers from catching cholera and other diseases by keeping their intestines warm. Four other bodies were also listed as wearing cholera belts.

The other female victim identified from personal effects in 1991 was Vendla Maria Heinen (Body No. 8), a Finn travelling third class to New York in search of work. Among her belongings was a chemise marked "V. H." in red on the front and 150 Finnish marks sewn into her clothing. Second-class saloon steward Alan Franklin (Body No. 262) of Southampton was also not identified until 1991,

A Celtic cross marks the grave of Australian Gordon McCrae, photographed in the 1920s. It is largest private headstone of all Titanic *burials in Halifax.*

despite wearing a shirt marked "A. Franklin" and a coat with a Southampton tailor's tag. The last victim to be identified in Row 1 has become the most well-known of all Halifax burials—the "Unknown Child." That story is told in the next chapter.

One of the identified crew members was Jock Hume, second violinist in the *Titanic's* musical ensemble (Body No. 193). On April 30, Hume's father received a letter from the Liverpool company that provided the musicians, requesting that he settle his son's outstanding balance of 14 shillings and 7 pence (about three-quarters of an old pound) for various items, including his uniform account. The contract Hume had signed stipulated that the cost of uniforms and any altera-tions made to them were to be paid by the musicians. Hume earned £4 a month.

Since Row 2 contains only five burials (one of which is unidentified), including the last body to be buried, it was probably the last row started. The headstone for second-class passenger Arthur Gordon McCrae (Body No. 209) is the biggest of all *Titanic* grave markers in Halifax. The large Celtic cross for the Australian engineer was paid for by his parents and carries the inscription "Faithful Unto Death." Finn Jacob Wiklund (Body No. 314), en route to Quebec with his older brother, Karl, is buried beside McCrae. Karl's body was not recovered. Next to Wiklund is a larger stone marking the grave of Harold Reynolds (Body No. 327), which was paid for by his parents. Reynolds, a baker, was on his way to Toronto. His body was found clinging to a life preserver by *Montmagny*. Among the inscriptions on his marker are a reference to the hymn "Nearer My God to Thee" and the quote "In The Midst Of Life We Are In Death." At the end of the row, the badly decomposed body of first-class saloon steward James McGrady (No. 330) was buried on June 12. He was the last victim found by a contracted ship.

Row 3 contains thirty-one burials and curves slightly at the top towards Row 1. Seven of these were unidentified until 1991. Of the identified, only three are pas-sengers and twenty-one are crewmen. One of the identified passengers is George Swane, the Allison family chauffeur. His body (No. 294) was one of the last recov-ered. Among the crew members, perhaps no grave received more attention for a time than that of Joseph Dawson (Body No. 227). Listed on the headstone as "J. Dawson," the coal trimmer has become identified with director James Cameron's character Jack Dawson, played by Leonardo DiCaprio, in the blockbuster 1997 movie *Titanic*. When the movie was released, the grave became an object of intense interest.

Like fellow steward John Hart, William Cox (Body No. 300) led several third-class passengers to safety from below deck. Although his remains were identified at the time, his name was not added to his headstone until 1991. His bravery remains unrecorded.

Not only well-off families paid for larger headstones. The marker for assistant second-class steward George Dean, while the same shape as the standard one, is larger and carries additional inscriptions, including "Aged 19 Years" and "Very Deeply Mourned By His Sorrowing Parents Fred & Mary Dean." His body number (252) is not on the stone, which is the only non-standard one in Row 3.

Row 4 has forty-eight burials and has a pronounced curve towards Row 1, supposedly to represent the bow of a ship. Additionally, there is a gap between the ends of Rows 1 and 4, which some maintain symbolizes the gash in *Titanic's* hull caused by the iceberg, although there is no record of Christie's intention in doing this. It could be that Christie was simply making best use of the slope of the land available to him. The first grave in Row 4 is that of Luigi Gatti (Body No. 313), manager of *Titanic's* first-class à la carte restaurant and cafe. Most of his staff were from his two London restaurants, Gatti's Adelphi and Gatti's Strand. All of them were either Italian or French and ten of them were his cousins. Gatti had been on *Olympic* when she collided with HMS *Hawke* and his wife asked him not to sail on *Titanic's* maiden voyage. In response, he told her not to worry because he was a good swimmer.

John Chapman (Body No. 17) was a second-class passenger and farmer from Cornwall, England. He was identified from an embroidered "J. Chapman" on his handkerchief. Chapman had originally immigrated to Canada in 1906 and then settled in Spokane, Washington, four years later. He returned to Cornwall in 1911 and married Sarah Lawry on Boxing Day. Sarah's brother was a carpenter living in Wisconsin, so the newlyweds decided to immigrate and join him. Their *Titanic* voyage was to have been a belated honeymoon.

When the lifeboats were being loaded and Sarah realized that her husband would not be allowed to accompany her, she turned to a shipboard acquaintance who was about to enter Lifeboat 4 and said goodbye, adding, "If John can't go, I won't go either." Like her husband, Sarah died in the sinking but her body was never found. Incongruously, among John's possessions was a lady's handbag; perhaps Sarah had handed it to him to carry for her at the last minute. In the movie *A Night to Remember*, the portrayal of a newlywed couple in second class—Mr. and Mrs. Clarke—was based on the Chapmans. They have a conversation in the main lounge with Thomas Andrews, *Titanic's* designer, who gives them advice about leaving the ship as she goes under.

Two graves over from Chapman is that of Maprie Der Zakarian (Body No.

304), one of the group of six Turkish Armenians headed for Brantford, Ontario. Sarkis Mardirosian, Orsen Sirayanian, and Ortin Zakarian also perished in the disaster, but only Der Zakarian's body was recovered. The "Der" in his name is an honorific, indicating that he had an ancestor who was a priest.

J. Bruce Ismay paid for the headstone of Ernest Freeman, Titanic's *chief deck steward.*

Row 4 contains six larger headstones, the most of any row. That of assistant purser's clerk Ernest Waldron King (Body No. 321) carries additional information, including, "In Loving Memory Of," "Currin Rectory Clones, Ireland," "Died On Duty S.S. 'Titanic,'" "Aged 28 Years," as well as bearing the religious inscription "Nothing In My Hand I Bring, Simply To thy Cross I Cling."

Like William Harrison's, Ismay also paid for the large headstone of chief deck steward Ernest Edward Samuel Freeman (Body No. 239). It notes he was the "Last Surviving Son Of Capt. S.W. Kearney Freeman, R.N. Husband Of Laura Mary Jane Freeman" and that "He Remained At His Post Of Duty, Seeking To Save Others, Regardless Of His Own Life And Went Down With The Ship." A sub-base carries the inscription "Erected By Mr. J. Bruce Ismay, To Commemorate A Long And Faithful Service."

Three graves away, the larger, standard-shaped headstone of coal trimmer Everett Edward Elliott (Body No. 317) notes he was "Of The Heroic Crew S.S. 'Titanic.' Died On Duty" and carries the poignant inscription "Each Man Stood At His Post While All The Weaker Ones Went By, And Showed Once More To All The World How Englishmen Should Die." In the face of several newspaper stories about crewmen surviving while women and children died, Elliott's family wanted to ensure that people understood that he had died bravely doing his duty.

Two other crewmen in Row 4 have headstones similar to Elliott's. Gertrude Cave paid for that of her "Dearly Beloved Husband" Herbert (Body No. 218), a first-class saloon steward. It bears a religious quotation, the third verse from the hymn that many believed the ship's orchestra played as *Titanic* started her final plunge:

There Let My Way Appear
  Steps Unto Heaven
All That Thou Send'st To Me
  In Mercy Given
Angels To Beckon Me
  Nearer My God To Thee
Nearer To Thee.

Five graves away, the headstone of third-class steward George Frederick Talbot (Body No. 150) notes he was the "Eldest Son of George & Ada Talbot, Of Southampton, England" and also carries a religious inscription:

I've Anchored My Soul
  In The Haven Of Rest,
I'll Sail The Wide Seas No More
  The Tempest May Sweep
O'er The Wide Stormy Deep,
  In Jesus I'm Safe Evermore.

The last of the larger headstones is that of Alma Pålsson, who was presumed until recently to be the mother of the Unknown Child buried nearby at the top of Row 1. The next chapter contains the full story of the Unknown Child.

Alma Pålsson is buried close to the Unknown Child.

MOUNT OLIVET ROMAN
CATHOLIC CEMETERY

MOUNT OLIVET WAS established in 1896, on land that was originally part of the estate of the Archbishop's Palace. Nineteen victims were buried there, in two rows on level ground. Frequently the deciding factor in burying a victim in Mount Olivet was the discovery of crucifixes, religious medallions, or rosaries on the body. Medallions were often registered as charms, while rosaries were listed as beads.

Row 1 contains six indentified and four unidentified burials, three of whom were females. J. Fred Clarke (Body No. 202) was one of three musicians recovered. The Liverpudlian played bass viola in *Titanic*'s small orchestra and was making his first trip across the Atlantic. Body No. 5 was the earliest victim pulled from the ocean that has never been identified. It was a short, heavyset female,

Musician J. Fred Clarke was identified from this card found on his body.

estimated to be a third-class passenger. Because a crucifix was found among her belongings, she was buried in Mount Olivet Cemetery. Similarly, because Body No. 13 had a "charm" around her neck, which could have been a religious medallion, she was buried in the Catholic cemetery. Recorded as "Probably an Italian," there was little to identify her as her clothing bore no markings.

On the other hand, the effects found on Body No. 12 were quite extensive. Among the items found on the woman with black, greying hair were a rosary (listed as "bead necklace") and a religious medallion with the letters "B. V. M." (listed as "charm round neck"). B. V. M. stands for "Blessed Virgin Mary," which—along with the rosary—led to her burial in Mount Olivet. A box of pills found on the body bore the name and address of chemist James Fleming in Athlone, Ireland. In response to a query from authorities in Halifax, a letter from Fleming in August confirmed he had supplied the pills to a Mrs. Rice on April 9.

Margaret Rice was a third-class passenger returning to the United States from Ireland. Margaret and her husband, William, had emigrated to Montreal, where William worked as a shipping clerk for the Grand Trunk Railway. In 1909, they

Funeral services were held at St. Mary's Basilica for some of the Roman Catholic victims.

moved to Spokane, Washington, where he worked for the Great Northern Railway as a machinist. The next year, William was killed in an accident in a railyard and Margaret returned to Ireland with her five boys using the payout from his insurance policy. Margaret worked as a housekeeper in Ireland, but life in her homeland did not turn out to be what she had hoped. She decided to return to the United States, where she apparently thought there would be more opportunities for her children. Sometime after *Titanic* hit the iceberg, another third-class passenger saw Margaret holding Eugene, two, in her arms, while the other four boys clung to her skirts. The entire family died in the sinking; none of the boys' bodies were recovered. It was the single biggest loss for any of the emigrant Irish families aboard *Titanic*.

Row 2 contains nine burials. Originally one of them was unidentified, but in 1991 the victim was tentatively identified as Hileni Zabour (Body No. 328), a sixteen-year-old who was travelling third class from Syria with her older sister. Next to Hileni is the grave of first-class passenger Servando Ovies y Rodriguez (Body No. 189)—or perhaps not. When the body was recovered it was listed as "Probably a Sailor," based on his clothes and rough hands. Apart from a shirt marked "J. R.," there were no clues to his identity and the body was buried in Fairview Lawn on May 3. Others quickly claimed that the body was that of Ovies, from his family in Spain to the family firm of Rodriguez and Company in Havana, Cuba, where Ovies worked. When company executive J. A. Rodriguez positively identified the body from the written description as Ovies—a Catholic—it was exhumed and reburied in Mount Olivet on May 15. Speculation at the time suggested that the identification may have been made to comfort Ovies's mother in Spain and to settle matters of inheritance.

Also buried in Mount Olivet is Mansour Hanna (Body No. 188), one of the Syrian Lebanese who boarded at Cherbourg on his way to Ottawa. Nearby lay the remains of Petril (Peter) Lemperopolis (Body No. 196), a third-class passenger from Greece. His headstone is the only one of all 150 in Halifax to have inscribed on it the name Bishop, the stone carver responsible for making all the markers.

BARON DE HIRSCH CEMETERY

THE NEED FOR a Jewish cemetery in Halifax came to an urgent head in the 1890s when Morris Levy, one of the founding members of Baron de Hirsch Hebrew Benevolent Society (the original name of the Beth Israel Synagogue), died suddenly in March 1892. Levy's body had to be shipped to New York City for burial. To resolve this issue, other members of the society purchased a plot of land next to the site of the planned Fairview Lawn Cemetery for a Jewish cemetery. The cemetery was consecrated on July 30, 1893, and is known by two names: Baron de Hirsch Cemetery and Beth Israel Synagogue Cemetery.

German banker and philanthropist Baron Maurice de Hirsch was born in Munich in 1831. He established charitable organizations to promote Jewish education and improve the lot of fellow Jews elsewhere in Europe. He also founded the Jewish Colonization Association that sponsored the emigration of large numbers of Jews to Argentina, as he believed that Jews were originally an agricultural people and should return to their pastoral roots. During his lifetime, de Hirsch amassed a large fortune, much of which he gave away. After he died in 1896, his wife continued his charitable works. By the time she died three years later, it was estimated the two had donated more than $100 million to various causes.

RABBI WALTER

WHEN THE 190 bodies recovered by the crew of *Mackay-Bennett* were delivered on April 30 to the temporary morgue set up in Halifax's Mayflower Curling Club,

Alexander McDougall, superintendent of Fairview Lawn and Camp Hill Cemeteries, stands between stonemasons Frank Fitzgerald (left) and Frederick Bishop (right) at the Baron de Hirsch Cemetery after headstones have been installed on the Titanic *graves. Bishop received the contract to carve all* Titanic *headstones.*

Rabbi Jacob Walter had only three days to identify any Jews among the victims and make arrangements to bury them before sundown on Friday night, which marked the beginning of the Sabbath. For many victims, their religion was easily determined, but for others it was more problematic. On examination of the bodies, Walter found many who "looked" Jewish. In a bizarre move, on May 4 Walter unilaterally removed ten bodies that were waiting to be buried in the Fairview Lawn Cemetery, deciding that they were Jewish. The authorities had already issued the appropriate documents for these remains to be buried in Fairview and were not prepared to make any changes. By then, confirmation had been received that the remains were, in fact, the bodies of either Roman Catholics or Protestants and they were returned for burial to Fairview.

In the end, ten bodies—eight of which have never been identified—were buried in the Baron de Hirsch Cemetery in two rows of five. They are all males and seven of them (three stewards, three firemen, and a cook) were tentatively identified as crewmen by their clothing, badges, or ship's keys. No attempt was made to identify the eighth man as either passenger or crew. Although he wore a large amount of clothing, it was likely because he had either dressed for warmth or was trying to save his clothes. Unfortunately, none of the items (two pairs of pants, pyjamas, vest, suit, and overcoat) provided any help in identifying him.

COMPOUND MISFORTUNE

THE REMAINS OF Frederick Wormald (Body No. 144), a first-class saloon steward from Southampton, were recovered by *Mackay-Bennett* on April 24. He was buried in the Jewish cemetery because he had a Jewish-sounding name, but in fact he was an Anglican. Wormald left a wife, Emily, and six children behind, who were totally dependent on him for support. When his death and burial were confirmed, the White Star Line carried Emily and her children to New York aboard *Olympic*, *Titanic*'s sister ship, to visit his grave. On arrival in the United States, the family went

Because Catholic Michel Navratil sailed under the name of Louis Hoffman, he was presumed to be Jewish and is buried in Baron de Hirsch Cemetery.

to Ellis Island for immigration procedures—just like every other third-class passenger entering the country. Immigration officials either did not believe Emily's story or were completely unsympathetic to her plight, and rejected the family's attempt to enter the country on grounds of "no visible means of support." They were put back aboard *Olympic* and returned to Southampton.

Other passengers and the crew were so touched by their troubles that they collected more than £40 for the family. But further misfortune awaited the family in Southampton. When Emily and her children returned to their rented house after a six-week absence, they discovered their insensitive landlord had let it to another family. A next-door neighbour had managed to retrieve most of the Wormalds' possessions and store some in her house, while the larger pieces of furniture were stored with other neighbours. The next day they found new accommodation and shortly afterwards received money from the Titanic Disaster Fund that had been established to assist families.

The other identified body in Baron de Hirsch Cemetery is that of Michel Navratil, who was travelling with his two young boys. Their story is told in the next chapter.

Edmond and Michel, Jr. had been abducted by their father, Michel Navratil.

CHAPTER 10

SUFFER THE LITTLE CHILDREN

SAVED—AND LOST

IN CALCULATING THE TOTALS OF MEN, women, and children lost by class, many sources continue to maintain that no first-class children were victims of the *Titanic* disaster, using this statistic as another example of the class system at work. In fact, one first-class child did perish: three-year old Loraine, daughter of Hud and Bessie Allison of Montreal. The reason she is often not counted as a child is because she was listed as Miss Allison in the ship's documents, which befitted her status at the time as a first-class passenger. Loraine's fate is all the more tragic because at one stage she had actually been put safely into a lifeboat.

Bessie Allison with her children, Loraine and Trevor. Only Trevor survived.

The Allisons—Hud, Bessie, and Loraine—were travelling with Loraine's younger brother, Trevor, the children's nanny, Alice Cleaver, maid Sarah Daniels, cook Mildred Brown, and chauffeur George Swane. Beside Hud and Bessie's stateroom, Daniels shared a first-class cabin with Loraine, while Cleaver was with Trevor next door to Daniels. The cook and chauffeur were in second-class cabins next to each other on F deck, in shared accommodations. When *Titanic* struck the iceberg, a bedroom stewardess told Daniels to get dressed, but she immediately got back into bed once the stewardess left. She finally got up when a fellow passenger roused her and escaped in Lifeboat 8. Daniels did not take Loraine with her, so must have delivered the little girl to her mother first.

Meanwhile, when Hud left his cabin to find out what was happening, Cleaver took Trevor and went down to second class without telling anyone, apparently to rouse the cook and chauffeur. When Hud returned, Cleaver and Trevor were already gone, so he took his wife and daughter to Lifeboat 6, saw them safely into it, and then left, perhaps to search for Cleaver and Trevor. But when Bessie looked around and could not see Trevor, she left the boat with Loraine and set off in search of her baby. At that time, unknown to Bessie, Cleaver was already with Trevor, on the other side and at the other end of the ship, where they got safely away in Lifeboat 11. As mother searched frantically for child, it finally dawned on her that he must be in a lifeboat with his nanny. But by now it was too late and all the lifeboats had left. Because she would not leave the sinking ship without her daughter, Bessie Allison was one of only four first-class women lost in the disaster and Loraine the only child in first or second class to perish.

Shortly after the disaster, newspapers were filled with melodramatic stories of Bessie refusing to leave Hud's side or to enter the lifeboat without him. One account, allegedly from Daniels (which the newspaper described as Bessie's sister), noted, "The boat was full and she grasped Lorraine [sic] in one arm, her husband with the other, and stood waving her hand, and it seemed to me smiling as she saw us rowing away. The last I saw of her, just as the boat started to plunge to the bottom, was Bessie turning to her husband for a farewell kiss. As the water washed to their knees, Lorraine was holding to her mother's skirts." Sadly, the Allison family tragedy was not yet over. During a visit to his grandfather in Massachusetts in the summer of 1929, Trevor, just seventeen at the time, became ill due to food poisoning. Strong of body and mind, he insisted he was fine, refused to see a

Children's nurse Alice Cleaver holds Trevor Allison.

doctor, and took a train to Maine to join other relatives already vacationing there. Trevor's condition worsened and he died on August 7. His body was returned to Canada for burial in the Ontario cemetery next to the father he never knew.

While the Allison family tragedy was unfolding, down in second class their cook, Mildred Brown, was reluctant to get out of bed, despite the urging of George Swane and her roommates. Only when one of the roommates pointed out that she was probably the only person in the entire ship still in bed did she finally get up. In a letter to her mother written from *Carpathia* (she could not afford to send a telegram), the young cook noted, "No sooner was I on deck than I was bustled to the first class deck and pushed into one of the boats and I found nurse [Cleaver] and the baby [Trevor] were there." Swane, who saw Brown, Cleaver, and baby Trevor into Lifeboat 11, was not so fortunate and perished.

In 1940, a woman named Loraine Kramer bizarrely claimed to be Loraine Allison. She maintained that in those last panicky minutes aboard the doomed ship, her parents gave her to a man named Hyde (whom she alleged was Thomas Andrews in disguise, paid by Ismay to disappear so he could not testify about *Titanic's* speed!), who got away and brought her up in the American Midwest. Hud's brothers (who had inherited his $3-million estate as he died intestate) rejected her story and eventually she gave up on her claim.

TITANIC'S ORPHANS

LOUIS M. HOFFMAN had a secret. In the first place, that was not even his real name; it was Michel Navratil. Navratil was travelling with his two sons, four-year-old Michel, Jr., who was nicknamed "Lolo," and two-year-old Edmond, nicknamed "Momon." Originally from Slovakia, he had moved to Nice, France, in 1902 by way of Hungary. In 1907 Navratil married Italian Marcelle Caretto in London, England, while staying at the Charing Cross Hotel. By 1912, his attempt at operating a tailoring business was in difficulty and he accused Marcelle of having an affair. As a result, the couple separated and the children lived with their mother. The boys went to stay with their father on Easter weekend, but when Marcelle went to get them afterwards, her estranged husband had disappeared with their sons.

Navratil had decided to take the boys to America, in what may be the first documented case of international parental child abduction or kidnapping (the response to such action was only codified in 1980 by the Hague Convention on the Civil Aspects of International Child Abduction). They boarded a steamer in nearby Monte Carlo and sailed to England, where they stayed in London—coincidentally at the Charing Cross Hotel. There, Navratil purchased second-class tickets for *Titanic* under the assumed name of Hoffman, the real name of a friend who had helped them get away, while the boys were booked as Loto and Louis. Aboard the ship, he intimated that Mrs. Hoffman was dead and rarely let the boys out of his sight.

After *Titanic* hit the iceberg, Navratil dressed his sons with the help of another passenger and went up to the boat deck. By then, the bow was well under water and only three Collapsibles were left: A, B, and D. Only D could be launched properly from a davit, as A and B were still tied to the roof of the officers' quarters and could only be floated off as the water rose. To stop panicked passengers from storming the lifeboat, Second Officer Charles Lightoller ordered a human chain of crewmen around it, with orders to let only women and children through. Navratil passed the two boys through the ring, where some women wrapped them up to keep them warm. Although Collapsible D could take forty-nine people it was launched with only forty, despite there being more than fifteen hundred people still aboard *Titanic*. When *Carpathia* arrived on the scene, the boys had to be hoisted aboard in burlap sacks. On the ship, the boys could not identify themselves and spoke only French. First-class survivor Margaret Hays, who spoke French fluently, looked after them. She continued to care for them in her New York City home, under the auspices of the Children's Aid Society.

This photograph of the Navratil boys was carried in newspapers around the world and led to their identification.

As Michel, Jr. and Edmond were the only children to survive without a parent or a guardian, no one knew the real identity of the boys; they were called the "Orphans of the *Titanic*" by the press. Newspapers picked up their story and their photograph was published in North America and Europe. Marcelle saw the photograph and was brought to America, sailing from Cherbourg on *Oceanic*, courtesy of the White Star Line. It was during that voyage that *Oceanic* came across *Titanic*'s Collapsible A containing three badly decomposed bodies on May 13 (chapter 7). In New York, Marcelle was reunited with her sons and three days later returned to France with them aboard *Oceanic*, again with free second-class passage from the White Star Line.

Michel Navratil's body (No. 15) was one of the first recovered, and he was found with a loaded revolver in one of his pockets. As his second-class ticket identified him as Hoffman, it was assumed that he was Jewish and he was buried in the Baron de Hirsch Cemetery. Even when his true identity was discovered and it was determined he was in fact Catholic, his body was left in the Jewish cemetery, although his real name was inscribed on his headstone. Back in France,

Edmond became an interior decorator and then an architect. During the Second World War, he served in the French army, was captured, and later escaped. The experience affected his health, however, and he died in 1953, only forty-three years old. His mother outlived him and died in 1974.

Michel went to college, obtained a doctorate, and became a philosophy professor. He maintained that his brush with death and loss of his father at an early age influenced his thinking for the rest of his life, calling himself a "fare-dodger of life. A gleaner of time." He visited the United States for the first time since the tragedy in 1987, on the seventy-fifth anniversary of the sinking. In 1996 he travelled to Halifax and saw his father's grave. Although only four years old when *Titanic* sank, Michel claimed that he could recall his father's parting words: "My child, when your mother comes for you, as she surely will, tell her that I loved her dearly and still do. Tell her I expected her to follow us, so that we might all live happily together in the peace and freedom of the New World." Michel died in 2001 at ninety-two, the last male survivor of the tragedy.

THE UNKNOWN CHILD

THE FOURTH BODY found by the crew of *Mackay-Bennett* resulted in one of the most endearing and enduring stories of *Titanic's* tragedy. The body was described as "Male. Estimated age, 2. Hair fair," while clothing was listed as "Grey coat with fur on collar and cuffs; brown serge frock; Petticoat; flannel garment; pink woolen singlet; brown shoes and stockings." The final entry stated "NO MARKS WHATSOEVER. PROBABLY THIRD CLASS." Of all the bodies recovered, this was the only one without a lifejacket. The care with which the child had been dressed for the cold indicated a caring parent or parents, but aside from that there was nothing to identify the baby who quickly came to be called the "Unknown Child." Many people were so moved by the story of the beautiful little blonde boy that they offered to pay for his funeral, but so did the crew of *Mackay-Bennett* and it was they who were given the opportunity.

On May 4, all seventy-five officers and men of the cable ship attended the funeral at St. George's Anglican Church, more commonly known as the "Round Church" because of its design. The small white coffin bearing the tiny body was carried into the church for the service conducted by the Reverend Kenneth Hind, who had been on *Mackay-Bennett* when the body was recovered. After the service, a solemn procession journeyed to the Fairview Lawn Cemetery along streets lined with Haligonians. It was the only *Titanic* burial on that day. The

The funeral for the Unknown Child was held at St. George's Anglican Church on May 4.

Unknown Child's identity was the subject of intense speculation. Passenger lists were searched in an attempt to solve the puzzle. Only Loraine Allison had been lost in first class, while there were none lost in second class. That left third class as the only possibility. Fifty-two third-class children died, although many could be eliminated as the Unknown Child due to their ages, leaving perhaps less than half a dozen children to fit the description. Only the body of one young child was recovered; the next youngest victim recovered was that of a nine-year-old Walter van Billiard.

By May 13, authorities had listed Body No. 4 as "Baby? Paulson" and shortly afterwards as Leonard Paulson. Two-year-old Gösta Leonard Pålsson was travelling from Sweden with his mother, Alma, and three older siblings to the United States to join their father, Nils, who had immigrated to Chicago in 1910 and obtained employment as a tram conductor. Alma also had two brothers who lived in Chicago. The family boarded *Titanic* at Southampton. When the ship hit the iceberg, it took Alma quite a while to dress the children and the family arrived on the boat deck after the lifeboats had already left. There she ran into August Andersson (a Swedish socialist travelling under the name of Wennerström), whom she had met earlier in the voyage. Alma often played a mouth organ to entertain her children and Andersson reported that she played it on deck to calm them. He also held two of the children as Alma had asked, but when the waters rose, he lost his grip on them and they disappeared. Andersson managed to survive in Collapsible A, while all five Pålssons perished in the sinking. Nils held out hope that stories of a rescued child might refer to one of his, but was finally told by a White Star Line official in Chicago that they were all missing. The agent reported that Nils's "grief was the most acute of any who visited the offices...but his loss was the greatest. His whole family had been wiped out."

Gösta easily fit the description of the Unknown Child. Despite this identification, the stone placed over the grave (also paid for by the crew of *Mackay-Bennett*) reads "Erected To the Memory Of An Unknown Child Whose Remains Were Recovered After The Disaster To The Titanic April 15th 1912." Over the years it has come to symbolize all fifty-three children who died in the tragedy, most of whose remains were never recovered. Fittingly, the headstone is one of few not to bear a number. Alma's body (No. 206) was recovered with the tickets for all four children and buried—many believe appropriately—very close to the Unknown Child. Her headstone (with her name spelled as Paulson) lists the names of her two girls and two boys in descending order of age: "Torburg Danira Aged 8, Paul Folke Aged 6, Stina Viola Aged 4, Gosta Leonard Aged 2."

In 2001, a request from the relatives of victim Catherine Wallis to inscribe her name on a tombstone eventually led in a round-about way to the positive identification of Body No. 4. As the description the family gave of their relative (Body No. 281) did not match the original coroner's report, DNA testing was suggested as a means of confirming her identity. At the same time, the presumed relations of two other bodies, the Unknown Child and Body No. 240 (thought to be Charles Shorney) were asked if they would agree to DNA testing and the provincial medical officer signed the exhumation orders. Although several Haligonians objected to what they thought was an unnecessary disturbance of these graves, the exhumations began on

Two-year-old Gösta Pålsson was presumed to be the Unknown Child for many years.

May 17, with assurances that proper protocols would be followed for handling the remains. When the graves of Body Nos. 240 and 281—which are side by side near the beginning of Row 1—were opened, workers discovered nothing inside.

Although the grave of the Unknown Child contained few remains, a six-centimetre fragment of an arm bone and three teeth were found and sent to the department of anthropology at Lakehead University for DNA analysis. The department's paleo-DNA laboratory, which applies molecular genetics techniques to the study of degraded human remains, has an international reputation. On the outside of the top of the coffin a medallion was found that read "Our Babe." It was returned to the grave.

Under Lakehead adjunct professor Ryan Parr, a team extracted mitochondrial DNA—which is passed from mother to child—from the remains and compared it with samples from maternal relations of Gösta. Alan Ruffman of Halifax, a *Titanic* researcher and author, had tracked down the relatives and obtained permission for the samples. None of it matched. Parr and his associates then broadened their search to include five other boys under the age of three who

Halifax police officer Clarence Northover was responsible for burning the clothing of Titanic's victims, but could not bring himself to destroy a small pair of children's shoes.

had died in the sinking: Gilbert Danbom (five months) from Sweden, Alfred Peacock (seven months) and Sidney Goodwin (nineteen months) from England, Eino Panula (thirteen months) from Finland, and Eugene Rice (twenty-four months) from Ireland. Ruffman, who became involved in the project as a research associate of the Maritime Museum of the Atlantic in Halifax, had the challenging task of finding descendants of these five young boys. He persevered, and with the assistance of the family members, genealogists, researchers, historians, librarians, translators, and archivists tracked down their maternal lines and got permission to extract DNA samples. Individuals from all six families who may have been related to the child cooperated fully in the project, including a maternal relative who provided a blood sample shortly after his one hundredth birthday.

Three of the boys—Danbom, Peacock, and Rice—were quickly ruled out as non-matches, leaving Panula and Goodwin as possible matches. Expert analysis of the three teeth, based on their shape and condition, suggested an age somewhere between nine and fifteen months, eliminating Goodwin. On November 6, 2002, Parr and Ruffman announced that the results of both DNA and teeth analysis were consistent with the identity of Eino Viljami Panula, the thirteen-month-old Finnish boy, who was travelling with his mother and four brothers to Pennsylvania to join their father. All six family members were lost. About fifty researchers had assisted in this identification, including several from Brigham Young University in Utah, Arizona State University, and the University of Toronto. Later that year, relatives of Eino travelled to Halifax and visited the gravesite.

Despite this identification, doubts still remained—and it was a pair of tiny shoes that finally solved the mystery. Clarence Northover was a Halifax police officer who had helped guard the bodies, clothing, and personal belongings of the *Titanic* victims. To prevent souvenir hunters from scavenging articles of clothing, authorities had ordered them burned. Northover complied—except for one item. When he came to a pair of fourteen-centimetre-long brown leather shoes, he was overcome by emotion and kept them, hoping a relative would claim them. When that did not happen, he put them in his desk drawer at the police station. They remained there until he retired in 1918. Then, in 2005, Northover's grandson, Earle, donated the shoes to the Maritime Museum of the Atlantic. They were too big for a thirteen-month-old child to wear.

Ryan Parr and his forensic team took another look at the DNA evidence, assisted by the United States Armed Forces DNA Identification Laboratory located in Rockland, Maryland. This time, they focussed on another section of the DNA samples and in 2007 found another marker that pointed with 98.87 percent certainty to nineteen-month-old Sidney Leslie Goodwin. Their findings were published in the June 2011 issue of the journal *Forensic Science International: Genetics*. Sidney was travelling with his parents, Frederick and Augusta, as well as two older sisters and three older brothers ranging in age from nine to sixteen,

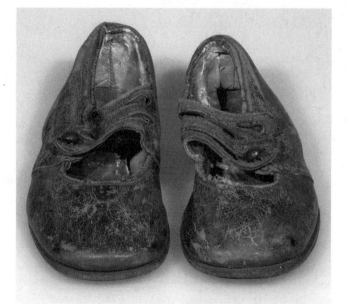

This pair of children's shoes, now on display in the Maritime Museum of the Atlantic, helped solve the mystery of the identity of the Unknown Child in 2011, ninety-nine years after the disaster..

from their home in Fulham, England, to Niagara Falls, New York. Frederick was an electrical engineer and had a brother who lived in Niagara Falls. The brother told Frederick about the opening of a new power station there, so Frederick decided to emigrate with his family in search of work. Originally the family was booked on *New York*, but had to switch to *Titanic* because of the coal strike. They were travelling third class to save money. The shoes show a lot of wear and were probably hand-me-downs from Sidney's older siblings. The entire family perished in the disaster, and Sidney's body was the only one recovered.

On August 6, 2008, Goodwin family relatives conducted a memorial service in Fairview Lawn Cemetery, convinced that Sidney Goodwin was the little boy whose remains were buried under the Unknown Child's tombstone. As a cousin read out the names of the children who died when *Titanic* sank, a bell was rung for each name. As the first name was read out, a light rain began to fall, and when the last name was spoken, it stopped. The Goodwins' relatives believe, as many others do, that the headstone of the Unknown Child continues to symbolize all the children who perished that night.

The u.s. Senate convened an inquiry into the Titanic *tragedy even before* Carpathia *had docked at New York with survivors. Once the ship arrived, J. Bruce Ismay (centre) was one of the first to testify.*

CHAPTER 11

AFTERMATH

THE INQUIRIES

BOTH THE UNITED STATES AND BRITAIN conducted inquiries into the loss of *Titanic*. The American one, headed by Senator William Alden Smith, was first. It started in New York on April 17 and ended in Washington on May 25, having sat for seventeen days. Although Smith wanted to discover what had happened and who was responsible, his biggest concern was why the sinking had occurred, in order to prevent a repetition of the tragedy. In New York, the hearings were held at the Waldorf-Astoria Hotel.

THE WALDORF-ASTORIA

The Astoria Hotel, part of the Waldorf-Astoria, which had been built by John Jacob Astor in 1897, was billed as "the world's most luxurious hotel." It was next door to the Waldorf Hotel, built four years earlier by his cousin, William Waldorf Astor. Later, the two hotels were connected by a ninety-metre-long corridor, which was quickly christened Peacock Alley because of the well-dressed members of the upper class who used to strut along it nightly. Together, the complex became known as the Waldorf-Astoria Hotel and was managed jointly. The original Waldorf-Astoria was demolished in 1929 to make way for the Empire State Building, while the modern hotel of the same name was opened on its present site in 1931.

The British were upset over what they considered American effrontery in holding an official inquiry concerning a British ship. But the Americans were entirely within their rights; although *Titanic* had a British crew, she was owned by an American company and destined for an American port. Smith's committee was unable to assign any blame for the disaster, but did make some important recommendations. Any vessel using an American port had to have enough lifeboats for all passengers and crew, lifeboats had to carry survival equipment and be manned by trained crews, and a lifeboat drill had to be held for every person on each voyage. These regulations came into effect immediately. With regard to wireless communications, all passenger-carrying ships had to be equipped with wireless, one company's transmissions could not be given precedence over any others, ship messages would take priority over private ones, and the wireless would have to be manned around the clock.

The British inquiry, called the Mersey Commission after its chairman, Lord Mersey, began on April 30 and ended on July 30. Its main aims were to discover why and how the sinking occurred. Its findings blamed the collision on excessive speed and lack of a proper watch, and also stated that the lifeboats were insufficiently manned. Both inquiries blamed Captain Stanley Lord of *Californian* for failing to come to *Titanic*'s aid after "distress signals" were seen from his ship. Between them, the two inquiries questioned dozens of passengers and crew. Not one passenger was from third class. J. Bruce Ismay appeared at both inquiries.

To the Americans he was a villain (one newspaper called him "J. Brute Ismay"), while the British treated him like a hero. When he died in 1937, his obituary in the *Times* (London) made no mention of *Titanic*.

Besides the changes ordered as a result of the American inquiry, other improvements quickly followed. *Titanic*'s sister ships underwent major upgrades. Along with her existing double bottom, *Olympic* had a double hull installed, as well as watertight bulkheads rising to the main deck, while *Britannic* (formerly *Gigantic*), which was still being built, had similar upgrades. Ships were now required to go around icefields instead of through them. In 1914 an International Ice Patrol was established to monitor icebergs, based on the U.S. Coast Guard. Every year since then the patrol has laid a wreath at the site of the sinking. The patrol, which is funded by seventeen nations, still performs its essential duties today, although aerial surveillance gradually replaced ship reconnaissance after the Second World War.

The British Merchant Shipping Act of 1894, the same law that decreed *Titanic* only needed to carry sixteen lifeboats, held White Star Line liable for $600,000 in freight losses. American law limited compensation up to the value of salvage—in this case, thirteen lifeboats—as well as reimbursement for the cost of

Titanic *lifeboats hang from the side of* Carpathia. *Until modern times, they were the only items salvaged from the great liner.*

the tickets for anyone who did not survive; a total liability of $97,772. The law in Britain allowed larger payments, however, and most lawsuits were transferred there. Claims for property filed against White Star totalled $16,804,112, ranging from $41.00 by the U.S. Postal Service to $177,352.74 submitted by Charlotte Cardeza for lost luggage. The largest claim for loss of life was for $1,000,000, filed by Irene Harris. It took until 1916 before the courts settled all lawsuits for a total of $663,000.

SURVIVAL STATISTICS

TO THIS DAY there is disagreement over how many people were aboard *Titanic* when she left Queenston, how many died, and—incredibly—even how many survived, with numbers of the latter varying between 701 and 713. The table opposite is a reasonable estimate, but it is highly doubtful that the exact numbers will ever be known. In any case, differences in numbers between various sources are relatively small.

Titanic *survivors recover aboard their rescue ship* Carpathia.

Survival Statistics

	Women	Saved	Lost	% Saved
Women	1st Class	140	4	97%
	2nd Class	80	13	86%
	3rd Class	76	89	46%
	All Passengers	296	106	74%
	Crew	23	3	87%
	Total	319	109	75%
Children	1st Class	5	1	83%
	2nd Class	24	0	100%
	3rd Class	27	52	34%
	Total	56	53	51%
Men	1st Class	57	118	33%
	2nd Class	14	154	8%
	3rd Class	75	387	16%
	All Passengers	146	659	18%
	Crew	192	695	28%
	Total	338	1354	20%
Total	1st Class	202	123	62%
	2nd Class	118	167	41%
	3rd Class	178	528	25%
	All Passengers	498	818	38%
	Crew	215	698	24%
	Total	713	1516	32%

No city in the world was more heavily affected by the Titanic *tragedy than Southampton, where the majority of her crew lived. The disaster left more than five hundred widows and fifteen hundred orphans in the port city.*

TITANIC ERRORS AND OMISSIONS

THE TRAGEDY OF *TITANIC* was caused by a combination of many factors, several having to do with the ship's lifeboats. Although the huge ship carried more than legally required, the lack of sufficient lifeboats immediately strikes the casual observer as a key error. But there were at least seven other errors made in association with the lifeboats: Captain Smith cancelled the mandated drill for Sunday, the day *Titanic* hit the iceberg; filling the lifeboats did not start early enough or with any degree of urgency; too many crew members were unfamiliar with the operation of the lifeboats; not all lifeboats were filled to capacity (apparently over fears they would collapse due to the weight), except for three lowered partway through the process; Second Officer Lightoller generally would not allow men or older boys into the lifeboats he controlled; a number of third-class passengers were held below for too long before they were allowed on the boat deck; and, once lowered away, only one lifeboat returned in time to pick up additional people, either directly from the ship (as some had been ordered to do) or among those struggling in the freezing water.

But problems with the lifeboats were not the only factors that contributed to the disaster. *Titanic*'s construction was faulty in two respects. Her hull steel was too brittle (although this was not recognized at the time), particularly at the temperatures encountered that night, and her watertight compartments did not go high enough. On being warned of ice, Captain Smith did not display sufficient caution. He continued to steam too far north at too high a speed at night with poor visibility. Compounding the visibility problem was the lack of binoculars for the crow's nest lookouts. Wireless operation at sea, a relatively new innovation, was more concerned with its commercial aspects than its potential for safety. In addition, the eight rockets fired from *Titanic* did not adhere to the internationally-recognized signal for distress by firing at one-minute intervals. Instead, they shot into the sky randomly for an hour—about one every seven to eight minutes—which by 1912 international regulations simply indicated that a ship was having navigational problems and other vessels should stand clear.

Finally, the hubris of the era—the excessive pride of the Edwardians at all levels of society—should be seen as a factor in the disaster. The early years of the twentieth century were regarded by many at the time as a Golden Age of technology and innovation. Humans believed they had tamed the elements and were their master. To them, it was the natural order of the world. Although no White Star Line official ever referred to *Titanic* as unsinkable, an article that appeared in the respected journal *Shipbuilder Magazine* described *Olympic* and *Titanic* as "practically unsinkable." The moniker stuck. At Southampton before *Titanic* sailed, second-class passenger Mrs. Sylvia Caldwell asked a deckhand, "Is this ship really non-sinkable?" "Yes, lady," he responded, "God Himself could not sink this ship."

FIRE, WATER, EARTH, AND AIR: HALIFAX AND DISASTER

THE ANCIENTS BELIEVED that everything was composed of one or more of four essential elements: fire, water, earth, and air. Throughout history, these "essential" elements have been the cause of countless disasters, and Halifax seems to have experienced more than its fair share. Major fires destroyed parts of the city in 1850, 1859, 1882, 1911, 1912, and 1939. In 1998, Swiss Air Flight 111 suddenly plunged into the ocean near picturesque Peggy's Cove outside Halifax, killing all 229 aboard. In September 2003, Hurricane Juan—the "storm of the century"—carved a path of destruction through Halifax, the most damaging tempest in the modern history of the city. It was followed in February 2004 by White Juan—the second storm of the century within five months—which dumped record amounts of snow on Halifax. But it is with water that Halifax's most tragic disasters are associated. The sinking of the White Star Line ships SS *Atlantic* and RMS *Titanic* were the worst transatlantic catastrophes of the nineteenth and twentieth centuries, respectively.

The Norwegian steamship Imo, *formerly the White Star Line vessel* Runic, *lies beached on the Dartmouth shore after the 1917 Halifax Explosion.*

THE HALIFAX EXPLOSION

Coincidentally, it was a former White Star Line vessel that played a key role in the greatest disaster ever to hit Halifax. On December 6, 1917, the Norwegian ship *Imo* collided with the French munitions ship *Mont Blanc* in the Narrows separating Halifax Harbour from Bedford Basin. The result was the largest man-made, non-nuclear blast in history, which killed almost two thousand people and injured nine thousand more (out of a population of less than fifty thousand), as well as levelling much of north end Halifax and Dartmouth, including damage to more than 14,600 homes. To compound the misery, that night a terrible blizzard hit the city. To relate this to a modern disaster, the 9/11 terrorist attacks of 2001 killed nearly three thousand people in a city with a population of eight million. The numbering system that had been developed for *Titanic* bodies, as well as same-numbered canvas bags for victims' personal effects, was also used for fatalities of the explosion. Additionally, the Halifax Explosion severely damaged the building housing the Mayflower Curling Club.

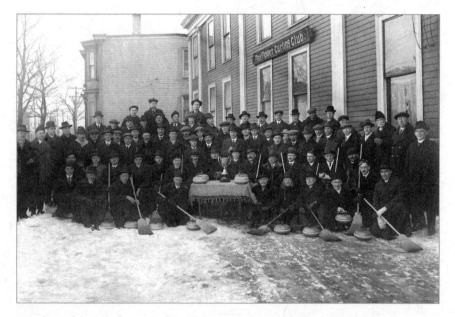

Members of the Mayflower Curling Club pose in front of their rebuilt clubhouse in 1920. It remained closed for more than a year after the Halifax Explosion.

Most of Titanic's *luxurious fittings have already deteriorated, but the memory of the terrible tragedy that struck her will endure.*

TITANIC ENDURES

AFTER THREE FAILED attempts at finding the wreck of *Titanic* in the early 1980s by Texan oilman Jack Grimm, it was finally discovered in 1985 by a joint Franco-American team under Jean-Louis Michel and Robert Ballard. Using data collected by Grimm's efforts, the new team was able to avoid searching areas already scanned by his expeditions. Early on the morning of September 1, the deep-towed ARGO camera/sonar combination transmitted pictures of *Titanic*'s boilers to the Research Vessel *Knorr* on the surface. *Titanic* had finally been found: 3,840 metres below the surface and almost twenty-two kilometres southeast of its last reported location. To everyone's surprise, she was sitting upright on the ocean floor, facing north. The bow and stern were about six hundred metres apart, at last confirming what several survivors had reported: *Titanic* broke in two before she went down. A massive debris field lay between the two sections. At first, Ballard believed that the wreck was safe from salvage-hunters because of its difficult accessibility and fragility. "*Titanic* will protect itself," he said.

But Ballard had not considered man's ingenuity. Even as he was making his announcements, Titanic Ventures was being formed to salvage artifacts. Initially, eighteen hundred (now more than six thousand) artifacts were recovered, which did not sit well with many scientists and *Titanic* enthusiasts. Then, an American court granted the company, now renamed RMS Titanic Inc., exclusive salvor rights to the wreck. RMS Titanic Inc. mounts exhibitions of its objects around the world; an amazing achievement that at one time no one would ever have thought possible. Several other deep-ocean submersibles have since visited the site, including tourist-carrying ones.

Eventually the day will come when little remains of *Titanic* on the ocean bottom. Many of her remaining artifacts will continue to be retrieved, while *Titanic*'s metal, wood, rope, cloth, leather, and other materials are deteriorating. Already almost all the wood is gone and "rusticles," created by a microbial process, are corroding the steel. Despite this deterioration and disappearance one thing will endure—the memory of the terrible disaster that struck the world's greatest ship.

APPENDIX

HALIFAX'S *TITANIC* LOCATIONS

MANY LOCATIONS IN HALIFAX are associated with *Titanic*. While most of them still exist, a few have disappeared. Among them are facilities associated with:

Transportation: Karlsen's Wharf, immediately north of the Halifax Casino at 2089 Upper Water Street, was the base for *Mackay-Bennett*. It formerly projected from the parking lot of HMCS *Scotian*, Halifax's reserve naval division, but was recently demolished. *Minia's* berth was at the Central Wharf, now under the towers of the Purdy's Wharf development, south of the casino. When *Mackay-Bennett* and *Minia* returned to Halifax with bodies from *Titanic*, they docked at the navy's Coaling Wharf No. 4, safe from prying eyes behind the naval dockyard's high stone wall. The wharf, long destroyed, was immediately north of today's Angus L. Macdonald Bridge. Relatives who came by train to identify bodies arrived at the Intercolonial Railway Station and remains that were shipped home for burial were sent from there. The station was located outside the dockyard main entrance on North Street, but was destroyed in the Halifax Explosion. The site is now a navy parking lot beneath the Macdonald Bridge.

Burial: Snow and Company Undertakers, responsible for all burial arrangements, stood at 90 Argyle Street (now 1740), today part of the Five Fishermen Restaurant. Next door was George A. Sanford and Sons Nova Scotia Steam Marble and Granite Polishing Works, which provided an undertaker to *Mackay-Bennett*. A bit further down Argyle Street stood Fred Bishop's Halifax Marble Works, which received the contract to supply the grave markers. An army surplus store now occupies 2660 Agricola Street (then 190), the site of the Mayflower Curling

Club, which was used as a morgue. Services for *Titanic* victims were conducted at St. Paul's Anglican (1749 Argyle Street), St. George's Anglican (222 Brunswick Street), All Saints Anglican (1330 Martello Street), Saint Mary's Catholic (5221 Spring Garden Road), and Brunswick Street Methodist churches. The original Brunswick Street church was destroyed by fire in 1979 and a United Church now occupies the site at 2107 Brunswick Street. St. Paul's curate Samuel Prince, who sailed on *Montmagny* in search of bodies, lived at the Grand Central Hotel, formerly on the southwest corner of Argyle and Prince streets. The Fairview Lawn (corner Windsor Street and Kempt Road) and Baron de Hirsch (Windsor Road) Cemeteries are next to each other, although the Jewish one is only open by appointment. Nearby, Mount Olivet Cemetery is on Mumford Road. Halifax's lone *Titanic* survivor, Hilda Lacon (née Slayter), is buried in a family plot in Camp Hill Cemetery (bounded by Robie Street, Veterans' Memorial Lane, and Summer Street). A bit further afield, survivor Alice Allen (née Fortune) is buried in the

Several of Snow's workers pose outside the undertaker's business with a horse-drawn hearse, 1910.

south shore community of Chester. Alice and her husband lived in Montreal and had a vacation home in Chester. They enjoyed their time in the village so much that they chose to be buried there.

Houses: The house in which Hilda Slayter grew up was a short distance from Snow's Funeral Home and still stands as St. Paul's Parish House (1706 Argyle Street). Halifax millionaire George Wright's architecturally significant Queen Anne Revival–style house (989 Young Avenue), which he bequeathed to the local Council of Women, is used by them to this day. Nearby is Wright's integrated housing development. On South Park Street between Morris Street and Holy Cross Cemetery are some of his upper-class houses, while around the corner on Morris Street are ones he built for the middle class, and in Wright Court, a short cul-de-sac off Morris Street, are row houses for the working class. Captain William deCarteret, commander of the Cable Ship *Minia*, rented one of the South Park Street houses.

Commercial buildings: Besides his housing development, Wright owned several other pieces of Halifax real estate. Two of his office buildings remain on Barrington Street, the Wright Building (1672) and the St. Paul's Building (1684). The White Star Line agency building is gone, but its facade remains, directly across from the Halifax Club (1682 Hollis Street). The long gone Halifax Hotel operated an information office with the latest news on recovery operations and many relatives undoubtedly stayed there. It stood on the site of the Ralston Building (1557 Hollis Street).

Institutions: The Maritime Museum of the Atlantic (1675 Lower Water Street) houses an outstanding exhibit, "*Titanic*: The Unsinkable Ship and Halifax," which showcases the museum's unique *Titanic* artifact collection, in particular wooden objects. The Nova Scotia Archives (6016 University Avenue) hold the original documents concerned with the recovery of *Titanic* bodies, including descriptions, lists of personal belongings, coroner's reports, and correspondence with families. After *Titanic* was discovered in 1985, the Bedford Institute of Oceanography in Dartmouth conducted research on *Titanic*'s rusticles and the first tests of her steel plating.

Memorials: The YMCA (1565 South Park Street), which benefitted from Wright's estate, displays a plaque commemorating a meeting room built in his memory. A monument to Wright was erected by his brother in Dartmouth's Christ Church Cemetery on Victoria Road.

BIBLIOGRAPHY

Adams, Simon. *Titanic*. New York: Dorling Kindersley, 1999.

Beed, Blair. *Titanic Victims in Halifax Graveyards*. Halifax: Nimbus, 2010.

Boileau, John. *Samuel Cunard: Nova Scotia's Master of the North Atlantic*. Halifax: Formac, 2006.

Butler, Daniel Allen. *"Unsinkable": The Full Story of the RMS Titanic*. Cambridge, Mass.: Da Capo, 2002.

Cochkanoff, Greg and Bob Chaulk. *SS Atlantic: The White Star line's First Disaster at Sea*. Fredericton: Goose Lane, 2009.

Davie, Michael. *The Titanic: The Full Story of a Tragedy*. London: Bodley Head, 1986.

Eaton, John P. and Charles A. Haas. *Titanic: Triumph and Tragedy*. New York: W. W. Norton, 1986.

Encyclopedia Titanica. www.encyclopedia-titanica.org.

Hustak, Alan. *Titanic: The Canadian Story*. Montreal: Véhicule, 1998.

Jeffers, Alan & Rob Gordon. *Titanic Halifax: A Guide to Sites*. Halifax: Nimbus, 1998.

Lord, Walter. *A Night to Remember*. London: Penguin, 1976.

———. *The Night Lives On*. New York: William Morrow, 1986.

Merideth, Lee W. *1912 Facts about Titanic*. Sunnyvale, Cal: Rocklin, 2003.

Pellegrino, Charles. *Ghosts of the Titanic*. New York: Avon, 2000.

———. *Her Name, Titanic: The Untold Story of the Sinking and Finding of the Unsinkable Ship*. New York: Avon, 1988

Ruffman, Alan. *Titanic Remembered: The Unsinkable Ship and Halifax*. Halifax: Formac, 2001.

Shapiro, Marc. *Total Titanic*. New York: Pocket Books, 1998.

Titanic. www.titanic-titanic.com

Wade, Wyn Craig. *The Titanic: End of a Dream*. New York: Rawson, Wade, 1979.

Wormstedt, Bill, Tad Fitch and George Behe. Titanic: The Lifeboat Launching Sequence Re-Examined. www.wormstedt.com/Titanic/lifeboats/lifeboats.htm, 2010.

IMAGE CREDITS

Blair Beed: 19, 25r, 35, 61, 74, 105, 112, 117, 121, 129, 130, 135, 137, 139, 145.
John Boileau: 1.
Maritime Command Museum: 108.
Maritime Museum of the Atlantic: 89, 101, 106, 134, 147, 162.
McCord Museum: 21l.
Nova Scotia Archives: front cover, ix, x, xi, 2, 3, 4, 6, 9, 10, 13, 17r, 25l, 29, 32l/r, 38, 39, 41, 43, 44, 49, 58, 59, 65, 71, 72, 73, 80, 81, 84, 85, 87, 88, 95, 96, 97t/b, 98, 99, 107, 109, 110, 111, 113, 119, 123, 124, 126, 131, 132, 143, 146, 151, 152, 154, 156, 157, 158, 162, back cover.
Private collection: 7.
The Sinking of the Titanic (1912): 17l, 18l/r, 21r, 30, 45, 47, 50, 54, 56, 63, 68, 75, 77, 78, 79, 91l/r, 102, 149.
Wikipedia Commons: 138, 141.

INDEX

International Mercantile Marine
Company 4, 12, 18
Ireland 35
Ismay, J. Bruce 4–5, 11, 12, 55, 69, 149,
150–51
Ismay, Thomas 3, 4

J

Jackman, John 100
Jackson, Edith 25
Jessop, Violet 63
John Elder and Company 84
John Snow and Company 86
Johnson, Peter 100
Joughin, Charles 69, 71
Jupe, Herbert 92

K

Karlsen's Wharf 161
Keefe, Arthur 103
Keeping, Edwin 18, 90–91
Kerley, W. T. 105
Kfar Mishki, Lebanon 34
Khalil, Solomon 34
Killam, Dorothy 117
King, Ernest Waldron 129
Kipling, Rudyard xii
Kirkland, Reverend Charles 36
Kramer, Loraine 139
Krekorian, Neshan 35, 69

L

Lacon, Hilda. *See* Slayter, Hilda
Lafargue, Juliette 33
Lakehead University 145
Larnder, Frederick Harold 84, 89, 110
Laroche, Joseph 33, 63
Laroche, Juliette 63, 120
Laroche, Louise 63
Laroche, Simone 63
Lawrence, Arthur 121
Lawrence, Lily 121
Lawry, Sarah 128
Lee, Reginald 42, 65
Lemperopolis, Petril (Peter) 133
Leslie, Shane 103
Lesueur, Gustave 31
Levy, Morris 133
Lightoller, Charles 10, 47–48, 51–52,
63, 66, 71, 74, 77, 103, 140, 155
Lily, D. 94. *See also* McElroy, Hugh
Liverpool, N.S. 69
Livshin, David 101–2

Lord, Stanley 42, 150
Lord, Walter 11
Lowe, Harold 10, 55, 63, 78, 101, 103
Lusitania 5, 32
Lyons, William 101–2

M

Mackay-Bennett, CS 83–89, 92–94,
107–9, 142, 161
Mallet, Albert 34
Mallet, André 34
Mallet, Antoinette 34, 120
Mallet, Antonine 67
March, John 121
Mardirosian, Sarkis 35, 129
Maritime Museum of the Atlantic xii,
98, 118, 147, 163
Mauretania 5, 23, 26
Mayflower Curling Club 108, 111, 112,
157, 161
Mayné, Berthe 34, 61
McCaffry, Thomas 23, 119
McConnell, John 21
McCrae, Arthur Gordon 126, 127
McElroy, Hugh 11, 69, 93
McGowan, Katherine 36
McGrady, James 100, 127
McQuillan, Fr. Patrick 100
Mersey Commission 150
Michel, Jean-Louis 159
Millet, Francis David 17
Milling, Jacob 120
Minahan, Daisy 36
Minahan, Dr. William 35, 36, 63
Minahan, Lillian 36, 63
Minia, CS 94–99, 161
Mitchell, P. V. G. 125
Moen, Sigurd 120
Molony, Senan 51
Molson, Harry 24, 61
Mont Blanc 157
Montmagny 99–100
Moody, James 10, 42, 71
Morgan, J. P. 12
Morrow, Thomas 36
Mosher, Dr. William 96
Mount Olivet Roman Catholic
Cemetery 131
Mount Temple 79
Murdoch, William 10, 42, 48, 51, 57,
60, 65, 66, 69
Murray, Maud 113–14

N

Nancarrow, William 114
National Line 3
Navratil, Edmond 137, 140–42
Navratil, Michel 135, 136, 140–42
Navratil, Michel Jr. 137, 140–42
"Nearer My God to Thee" 122
Newell, Arthur 112
Newell, Frank 112
New York 27–28
Nicholls, Joseph 91
Nicola-Yarred, Elias 34, 69
Nicola-Yarred, Jamila 34, 69
Niobe, HMCS 108
Nirva, Iisakki 27
Nomadic 29–30
Northover, Clarence 146, 147
Novel, Mansour 34, 92
Nye, Elizabeth 64

O

Oceanic 102
Oceanic Steam Navigation Company.
    See White Star Line
Olympic, ss 5–6
O'Neill, Annie 111
O'Sullivan, Brigit 36
Ottawa, ss 105

P

Pålsson, Alma 20, 130, 144
Pålsson, Gösta Leonard 144–45
Pålsson, Nils 144
Panula, Eino 146
Panula, Maria 20
Parisian 46
Parr, Ryan 145, 147
Payne, Vivian 23, 57
Peacock, Alfred 146
Pëde, Mathilde
    See Weisz, Mathilde
Perkis, Walter 67
Pernot, René 31
Perreault, Anne 23, 57
Peuchen, Arthur 10, 24, 61, 119
Phillips, Jack 11, 42, 44, 70, 71, 74, 102
Pirrie, Lord William 5
Pitman, Herbert 10, 55
Pouliot, François-Xavier 99
Prince, Rev. Samuel 100, 162
Pusey, Robert 60

Q

Queen Elizabeth 11
Queenstown, Ireland 35

R

Reynolds, Harold 127
R. H. Macy and Company 16
Rice, Eugene 133, 146
Rice, Margaret 131, 133
Rice, William 131, 133
Richard, Emile 34, 67
RMS Titanic Inc. 159
Robbins, Victor 31
Robertson, Morgan 39
Robins, Alexander 114
Robins, Grace Charity 114
Robinson, James 93
Rodriguez, J. A. 133
Rodriguez, Servando Ovies y 33, 133
Roosevelt, President Theodore 16
Rosenshine, George 115
Ross, Hugo 23, 119
Rostron, Arthur 46, 64, 78–80, 101, 102
Rothschild, Maurice 117
Rowe, George 63, 69
Ruffman, Alan 145–46
Ryerson, Arthur 67

S

Sage, Annie 20
Sage, John 20
Sage, Will 91
Sägesser, Emma 31
Sardinian 92
Shorney, Charles 145
Siebert, Sidney 101–2
Sirayanian, Orsen 35, 129
Slayter, Hilda 36, 65, 162, 163
Smith, Edward J. 6, 10, 44–45, 47, 70,
    71, 155
Smith, Sen. William Alden 149–50
Snow and Company Undertakers 161
Snow, John Jr. 86, 88, 89, 100, 110
Snow, William 96
"Songe d'Automne". *See* "Autumn"
Southampton xi, 10, 14, 16, 28, 29, 37,
    38, 102, 136
Stead, William Thomas 17–18
St. George's Anglican Church 142–43
Straus, Ida 16, 57, 117
Straus, Isidor 16, 17, 57, 117
Straus Park 118

OTHER IMAGES *of our Past* BOOKS

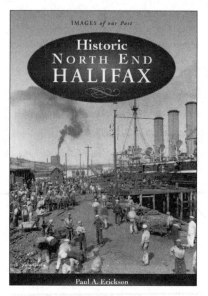

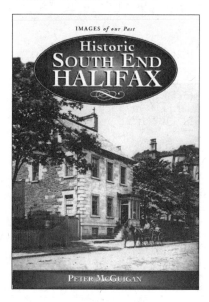

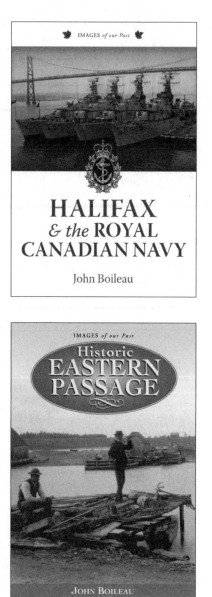